John Jackson

Mary Reed

Missionary to the Lepers

John Jackson

Mary Reed
Missionary to the Lepers

ISBN/EAN: 9783743332096

Manufactured in Europe, USA, Canada, Australia, Japa

Cover: Foto ©ninafisch / pixelio.de

Manufactured and distributed by brebook publishing software (www.brebook.com)

John Jackson

Mary Reed

MARY REED

MISSIONARY TO
THE LEPERS

BY
JOHN JACKSON
(Organizing and Deputation Secretary to the Mission to Lepers in India and the East.)

WITH INTRODUCTORY NOTE BY
REV. F. B. MEYER, B.A.

NINE ILLUSTRATIONS

SECOND EDITION.

London: Marshall Brothers
Paternoster Row, E.C
1899

Extract from Miss Reed's Letter, dated June 9th, 1899 :—

"SINCE the receipt of your letter, requesting a brief account of God's dealings with me, and of some of my experiences during 1897, 1898, and so far in 1899, I feel it to be my duty to give you some sketches from an almost blank diary, supplemented by something from a poor memory. This I consider a *duty* on my part, since your object is worthy *any* sacrifice any one could make. . . . . Never could I have been induced to sanction the publication you purpose sending forth on the blessed mission of interesting kind hearts in Christ's little ones, had I not realized during these years that I belong to Jesus ; and so I am glad to be used in *any way* for His service and in the advancement of His Kingdom."

LIST OF ILLUSTRATIONS.

	PAGE
PORTRAIT OF MISS REED	*facing title*
WILLIE RUSSELL (a leper)	,, 19
THREE INDIAN LEPERS	,, 29
A GROUP OF LEPERS BEING INSTRUCTED .	,, 45
A DESTITUTE LEPER	,, 59
A GROUP OF LEPERS AT CHAMBA, PANJAB .	,, 80
THREE BURMESE LEPERS	,, 92
A HOMELESS INDIAN LEPER	,, 105
A LEPER WOMAN IN PURULIA ASYLUM . .	,, 105

CONTENTS

	PAGE
EXTRACT FROM MISS REED'S LETTER	v
INTRODUCTORY WORDS BY REV. F. B. MEYER	ix

CHAPTER I.
EARLY LIFE 11

CHAPTER II.
DISCOVERY AND DECISION 15

CHAPTER III.
THE WAY OF THE CROSS 18

CHAPTER IV.
APPOINTED TO CHANDAG 22

CHAPTER V.
AMONG THE LEPERS 27

CHAPTER VI.
TRIALS AND TRIUMPHS—1894 32

CHAPTER VII.
PRAISE AND PROGRESS—1895 39

CHAPTER VIII.
A WELCOME VISITOR—1895 48

CHAPTER IX.
TRAVAIL OF SOUL—1896 57

CHAPTER X.
YEAR BY YEAR 64

CHAPTER XI.
CHRISTMAS WITH THE LEPERS 75

CONTENTS

	PAGE
CHAPTER XII.	
A VISION OF THE NIGHT	83
CHAPTER XIII.	
DIVIDED DUTIES—1897	91
CHAPTER XIV.	
LIGHT AND SHADE—1898	101
CHAPTER XV.	
THE PRAYER OF FAITH—1899	108

INTRODUCTORY WORDS.

ONE of the pleasantest episodes in my recent visit to India was the privilege of enjoying the hospitality of Miss Thoburn at Lucknow. One of her guests was Miss Mary Reed, with whom I had more than one delightful talk. This is my plea for writing a few introductory words to this record of her life and work.

She told me her wonderful story; how she first discovered that she was afflicted with the painful and loathsome disease of leprosy; tore herself away from those who loved her, without trusting herself to say good-bye; and finally consecrated her life to the relief of the lepers of India. From the first day until now she has borne her heavy cross in a spirit of consecration which makes the story of her life one of the most inspiring in missionary biography.

Next to sitting with her, and hearing the account of God's dealings with her from her own lips, is the opportunity of reading her story as told by the compiler of these pages, who has brought a sympathetic spirit and a full knowledge of the facts to aid him in the delineation of this noble life.

Not only does she never utter a murmuring word at her lot of suffering and isolation, or her environment of sin, disease, and death, but she joyfully acquiesces in what she accepts as God's will. She has already laboured for eight years amongst her fellow sufferers with evident tokens of the Divine approval. Necessarily debarred in a great measure from the privileges of intercourse with fellow workers, she has, in her lonely retreat amid the Himalayan snows, been cast the more utterly upon God and has proved that

" They who trust Him wholly
Find Him wholly true."

She has had the privilege of seeing the Institution under her care extend. Her afflicted flock has also increased in number; but, above all, she has had the rare joy of seeing many lepers welcomed into the fellowship of the Christian Church.

In a strength which is distinctly God-given, she labours on in faith and hope, receiving a present reward in the knowledge that in the deepest sense it is still true that the " Lepers are cleansed."

I cannot refrain from expressing my sincere admiration for Miss Reed's devoted spirit and Christ-like work, and I commend this little volume to all those who are interested in foreign missions, and trust that it may be the means of eliciting sympathy and support for the work of *The Mission to Lepers in India and the East*, of which Society Miss Reed is an honoured and valued worker.

F. B. MEYER.

CHAPTER I

EARLY LIFE

THE subject of this brief biography was born at Lowell, Washington County, in the State of Ohio (U.S.A.), and was the first girl in a family of four brothers and four sisters. Already blessed with a son, we may be sure the hearts of the parents accorded a warm welcome to their first little daughter. Happily, their joy was clouded by no prevision of the special lot of suffering awaiting her. In this quiet home, watched over by her parents, and surrounded by an atmosphere of love and happiness, the years of Mary Reed's childhood glided rapidly away.

When about sixteen, an age critical to the moral character, her nature was first awakened to the reality of the things that are not seen, but are eternal. As the young and supple seedling is bent to the shape that the sturdy oak bears in after years, so by the sweet constrainings of the Divine Spirit, the fresh young life was gladly yielded to her Saviour, and thus early was commenced the service which is now being consummated among her afflicted fellow-sufferers in India. From the time of her first surrender to the claims of Christ, she appears to have realized that she had been saved to serve, and that if she received, it was in order to bestow. An intense longing that others should share her newly-found joy induced her to engage earnestly in every form of Christian effort open to her. She was led to adopt the profession of a public school teacher, and for some ten years she pursued this calling with success, availing herself of the many opportunities her position afforded to impart to her pupils the knowledge of heavenly, as well as earthly, things. May we not see in this experience a providential preparation for the work in after years, of the organization and supervision of a large institution, peopled by those who, although men and women in years, she loves to speak of as her "little ones," or still more frequently as "Christ's little ones!"

But the Master had need of her for more difficult service than teaching work in America. She became conscious, dimly at first, of an inner voice pleading on behalf of her sisters in the Zenanas of India, still sitting in darkness and in the shadow of death. With the true humility which still characterizes her, she hesitated to believe that it was really a Divine call to leave all and follow whithersoever the Spirit led. But she was not disobedient to the heavenly vision. In spite of conscious weakness and a deep distrust of her fitness for such high and holy work, she cried at length, like Isaiah of old, " Here am I, send me," and also, like him, she heard the Divine command, " Go, and tell this people."

In connection with the Methodist Episcopal Church of America, there is an old-established and well-organized Women's Foreign Missionary Society, and to the Directors of this Miss Reed offered her services. They were gladly accepted, and her name was added to the roll of her sisters, then numbering 40 or 50, but since increased to 200, who are being supported by this

EARLY LIFE

earnest and energetic body. To the Cincinnati Branch fell the privilege of being represented by Mary Reed, and the loving but sad farewells having been said, she reached India in November, 1884. This surrender, on the part of the dear home circle, though it cost them many a pang, was endured for the Gospel's sake, and must, in some measure, have prepared them for the greater renunciation, then hidden in the darkness of the future.

At the Society's North India Conference in January, 1885, Miss Reed was allocated to Cawnpore, for work in the Zenanas of the city where the white marble angel marks the site of the well into which the treacherous Nana Sahib flung the bodies, dead and dying, of 125 English women and children. It is surely a Christ-like recompense that into a city stained within living memory with so foul a crime as this, Christian women should carry with prayer and patient labour the glad tidings of redeeming love. But not immediately was this herald of the Cross to proclaim her Evangel to the women of Cawnpore. At this juncture her health gave way, and a period of rest and change became imperative. In unconscious pursuance of the divinely ordered plan of her life, Pithoragarh, in the bracing climate of the Himalayas, was selected for the purpose. Here she spent a few weeks of earnest preparation for the work then awaiting her. In addition to study of the language, and observation of missionary work being carried on in the neighbourhood, she had an opportunity of seeing the very spot in which was to be erected (two years later), the Asylum over which she is to-day presiding with marked ability and success. Her pity was powerfully awakened on learning that within a comparatively small radius of this lovely spot, some five hundred lepers were to be found in a condition of utter misery and hopelessness.

With restored health, she gladly returned to Cawnpore to enter upon the work to which she had been appointed, and which for four years she was permitted to prosecute with zeal and energy, and not without tokens of success. No doubt this may be regarded as a further stage of training and preparation for the work, so peculiarly difficult from a merely human point of view, which the providence of God had assigned to her. From Cawnpore she was transferred to Gonda, where for twelve months she taught in the Girls' Boarding School. By this time her health was seriously undermined, and in January, 1890, she returned to America in search of renewed strength for further service.

CHAPTER II

DISCOVERY AND DECISION

IT was while resting in Cincinnati, some months after her return from India, that the real nature of her malady was revealed to Miss Reed. She had undergone a lengthy course of treatment, including at least one operation, but without the hoped-for restoration. Amongst the symptoms, which for some time completely baffled her physicians, were a constant tingling pain in the fore-finger of the right hand, and later, a strange spot on one cheek, near the ear. Then one day, with the suddenness of a flash, and the certainty of a voice, there was revealed to her, not only the *character* of her disease, but the *purpose* of it. Close upon the first feeling of dismay which must have accompanied so terrible a discovery, came a mental vision of the hopeless sufferers among the Himalaya mountains. It was borne in upon her, then and there, that *these* were to be the sheep of her flock, and *there* was to be the sphere of her future labours. After searching such medical books as she could lay her hands upon, she confided her suspicions to her physician and to one friend (the Cincinnati Secretary of her Society). Her fears were confirmed by her doctor, but as his knowledge of the disease was purely theoretical, he transferred his patient to New York as soon as she was fit for the journey. So this modern martyr set out upon her *via dolorosa*—her pilgrimage of suffering and isolation. In New York, she was examined by a specialist who had studied the disease in the Sandwich Islands. His verdict confirmed her own conviction, and this educated, refined, Christian woman found herself face to face with the appalling and paralyzing fact that she had fallen a victim to leprosy—the most dreaded, loathsome, and hopeless disease known to mankind.

Although this account of God's dealings with her is written by permission, it is also under the express injunction to "say not one word in praise of Mary Reed." Nor will we attempt to evade that restriction, but we will here invite the reader to unite with us and with her in admiring and extolling the DIVINE GRACE that has, from the first, enabled her to accept this heavy cross with entire resignation, and to say, in her own words, not with a sigh, but with a song—"Thy will be done."

Desiring to spare her family the pain the sad knowledge must have brought to them, and denying herself the motherly sympathy for which she must have yearned, she kept them, with the single exception of her sister Rena, in ignorance of what had befallen her. "If you will let me go without a special good-bye, as though I were returning to-morrow, it will be so much easier for me," she said. And so, self-debarred from even a farewell kiss, she went forth from that happy home-circle to become the centre and head of one of the saddest of all the families of suffering humanity.

Arrived in India, however, it became apparent to Miss Reed that the dear ones at home, for whose sakes she was prepared to suffer in silence, must shortly learn the sad truth. Accordingly, from Bombay she wrote:—

DISCOVERY AND DECISION

"After prayerful consideration, I find it wisest and kindest to tell you, or allow dear, brave-hearted sister Rena, with whom I entrusted this mystery of God's Providence, to tell you what she pledged to keep from you. She will tell you how our loving Heavenly Father, who is "too wise to err," has, in His infinite love and wisdom, chosen, called, and prepared your daughter to teach lessons of patience, endurance, and submission, while I shall have the joy of ministering to a class of people who, but for the preparation which has been mine for this special work, would have no helper at all; and while I am called apart among these needy creatures, who hunger and thirst for salvation, and for comfort and cheer, He, who has called and prepared me, promises that He, Himself, will be to me as a little sanctuary where I am to abide, and abiding in Him, I shall have a supply of all my need."

Surely the Grace of God shines forth here, and the strength of Christ is once more made perfect in human weakness. And the language of this letter, in which is revealed the view she was enabled to take of her affliction, is but the keynote of all her letters. Her confident faith in the presence and help of her Saviour has been abundantly justified. Strengthened with might by His Spirit, she has been enabled to say, in the words of one of her favourite hymns:—

> No chance has brought this ill to me,
> 'Tis God's sweet will, so let it be;
> He seeth what I cannot see.
> There is a need be for each pain,
> And He will make it one day plain,
> That earthly loss is heavenly gain.

CHAPTER III

THE WAY OF THE CROSS

FROM New York Miss Reed proceeded to London She brought with her letters of introduction to two eminent specialists, who both confirmed the decision of the American physician. During her brief stay in England, she was thrown into contact with a young countrywoman of her own, who was, moreover, as Miss Reed had been, a public school-teacher (from New England) and an earnest Christian. To her were permitted some days of close intercourse with this devoted sufferer which must have been inspiring as an experience, and must remain precious as a memory. I have the advantage of quoting from an account of these days, written by this sympathizing companion. She says: " I wondered instinctively at the ivory pallor of that sweet face, and at the cruel spot that disfigured it, so different from anything I had ever seen. I wondered, too, as the days went by, why the forefinger, always covered with a white cot, refused to yield to healing remedies." Miss Reed's suggestion that she should continue her journey towards Brindisi, in the company of the small party of whom her friend was one, was readily acceded to, although they doubted her ability to travel with the rapidity of the average American tourist, which was, perforce, their rate of progression.

WILLIE RUSSELL (an English Leper Boy) at the SABATHU ASYLUM, PANJAB.

Grateful as her sad heart was for this sympathetic companionship, so grateful that she said, "I think God has sent you here in answer to my prayer," she did not *yet* confide the knowledge of her secret sorrow to her friend. What a pathos the circumstances give to their visit to Canterbury! Centuries had passed since the last leper pilgrim had approached the tomb of the martyred Becket. Old historians have minutely recorded how in by-gone days all sorts and conditions of sufferers from this terrible scourge made their weary way hither in the hope of being healed. But if Mary Reed followed in the far off steps of Henry Le Pomerai, the wealthy Norman Knight, of the noble kinsman of Roderick, King of Connaught, and of the long procession of nameless and obscure sufferers whose knees wore away the stones of the shrine, it was not with the hope of leaving behind the heavy cross she had so bravely accepted. May we not say, as we believe she would say, that some better thing was reserved for her? To minister, as a very angel of mercy, to the souls and bodies of her fellow-sufferers with a sympathy, and with a success, perhaps only possible to one similarly afflicted, will, in the day of the "Inasmuch," be recognized as a higher good than even healing would have been. Describing their visit to Canterbury, Miss Reed's companion writes: "Under the smiling English skies we walked up to St. Martin's, the little church whose memories go back at least 1,300 years. Near the chancel, the English lassie, who guided us, stopped, and, pointing to an opening in the thick wall, said, "That is the lepers' squint." This was the orifice through which the poor sufferers, creeping to the sanctuary in olden times, were allowed to listen from without to the words of life, or behold what they could of the worship within. If I had known then what I knew afterwards, my heart would have bled for the woman at my side. Calmly she stood there before us with a heavenly light in her eyes, not a muscle of her face betraying her heart's secret."

During one of their hours of intimate intercourse, this friend, still unacquainted with the true motive for Miss Reed's return to India, ventured to question the wisdom of such a course in view of her evident bodily weakness. But it was a brave reply that came from the quivering lips: "My Father knows the way I go, and I am sure it is the right way." It was in Paris that this sister, whose sympathy had been so sweet to her suffering companion, was at length permitted to share her sad secret. The incident is best described in her own touching words :—

"On memory's walls there will hang while time lasts for me the picture of that scene. A wax taper burned dimly on the table beside her open Bible, that Book of all books from whose pages she received daily consolation; and while, without, Paris was turning night to day with light and music and wine, within, Mary Reed's gentle voice, faltering only at her mother's name and coming sorrow, told the secret of her affliction.

"As my throbbing heart caught its first glimpse of her meaning, I covered my face to shut out the swiftly rising vision of her future, even to the bitter end, and almost in agony I cried out, 'O, not that!—do not tell me *that* has come to you!' And when, in calmer moments, I said that every Christian ought to unite in prayer for her recovery, her only response was, 'I have not yet received any assurance of healing; perhaps I can serve my Father better thus.'

"I come with sorrow to my last evening with Miss

Reed. I sat in the shadow, and she, where the full moon rising over the snowy mountains just touched, with a glory that loved to linger, her pale, sweet face. Again I hear her voice in song:

> Straight to my home above,
> I travel calmly on,
> And sing in life or death,
> "My Lord, Thy will be done."

"And with the anticipation of our parting on the morrow, she told me of her last hours in her western home, of her father's farewell breathed out in his morning prayer, telling the All-Father and the heart of his daughter the sorrow that, for her sake, should be repressed; how, upheld by a strength not her own, she went out as if some day she might return, and then hastened on to the land of her exile.

"On the shores of lovely Lake Lucerne, hand clasped in hand for the last time on earth, and with eyes blinded by gathering tears, our farewell was whispered: 'God be with you till we meet again.'"

And in this spirit of consecration, and with the Christ-like resolve that her affliction should not hinder her usefulness, but rather triumphing over it, she went her way, alone, yet assuredly not alone, returning to India, as she herself had said, "under conditions in which no other missionary ever returned."

CHAPTER IV

APPOINTED TO CHANDAG.

IN September, 1891, the Mission to Lepers in India and the East was approached on behalf of Miss Reed, with a view to finding her a sphere of service among her fellow-sufferers. A letter from Bishop Thoburn, the Superintendent in India of the Methodist Episcopal Church, first informed the committee of this new worker who had been so strangely consecrated, but whose name was, for the time being, withheld. In writing to propose that Miss Reed be appointed Superintendent of the Asylum at Pithoragarh, Bishop Thoburn says: "It is a hard thing to say, and yet it does look as if Providence was sending her to a very needy people who otherwise could receive no help. The district in which Pithoragarh is located, that is, Eastern Kumáun, has more lepers in proportion to its population than any other district in India; at least, so the census indicates. It is a mystery how she ever contracted the disease. She accepts her fate in the best possible Christian spirit, and feels that she is set apart for the poor creatures who are similarly afflicted in Eastern Kumaun."

Shortly after this, the American newspapers, whose vigilance no private sorrow that will make "copy" can long evade, made public Miss Reed's name, together

APPOINTED TO CHANDAG

with such particulars as could be collected or invented. A deep impression was created on the mind of the Christian public, and much admiring sympathy was elicited.

In the meantime, while waiting the decision of the committee, Miss Reed found a welcome resting place at Pithora with Miss A. M. Budden, who, together with her sister and preceded by their devoted father, has done faithful service among the women, the children, and the lepers of that district. The large Leper Asylum at Almora, founded by the late Sir Henry Ramsay in conjunction with Mr. Budden, still stands as a memorial to the faithful services of these two, the Government Administrator and the Christian Missionary, who co-operated in its establishment and in its management for many years. From Pithora, under date of January 1st, 1892, Miss A. M. Budden wrote to Mr. Wellesley C. Bailey, Secretary and Superintendent of the Mission to Lepers : " I have been expecting to hear from you about the future arrangements for Miss Reed, who has come for shelter to Pithora as being the only place in the world that would shelter her. You will have heard that Miss Reed was for five years in this country as a Missionary of the Women's Foreign Missionary Society of the Methodist Episcopal Church, and went home in utterly broken health. It seems now that this complaint was coming on for some time before she left, and for a year after she arrived in America it was not suspected. At last the Lord Himself revealed it to her, and at the same time told her that Pithora was to be her future home, and that He had much work for her to do among those similarly afflicted. She informed the doctors of the nature of her complaint, and was sent by her own physician to see an expert in New York who confirmed her suspicions, and she was hurried out of the country before others were made aware of her complaint. She saw doctors in London and in Bombay—the doctor of the Leprosy Commission in the latter place—and all agreed that there was no doubt about the matter." After reference to the terms on which the charge of the work should be transferred to Miss Reed, Miss Budden continues : " You know there are more than 500 lepers in the Shor Pargannah alone, and the need of further assistance is very great. At present we are reducing rather than increasing, as we do not fill up vacancies caused by death—but oh! such *piteous* cases as have to be refused. After hearing Miss Reed's account of the wonderful way in which the Lord revealed His will to her about herself, and about Shor, it seemed to me that the day for ample help to these poor creatures had dawned, and I still believe it has. He who has led His servant by such an *awful* valley of the shadow of death to come here to serve Him thus, will surely touch hearts to supply the pecuniary assistance necessary to carry out His plans . . . . Miss Reed suffers constantly and most patiently. She feels that she has had her life call to work among these poor creatures, and, I believe, will end her days among them. She is highly sensitive, and of all my acquaintances I know of *no* one who would *naturally* more loathe this complaint, and yet to her it has been given! It is very, very wonderful, and so is His grace that enables her to bear it without a murmur, though often with scalding tears and a breaking heart. I feel it to be a special mark of my Master's favour that I am permitted to be the one to shelter and care for her."

The sisterly sympathy so fully extended to Miss Reed

APPOINTED TO CHANDAG

at Pithora must have been one of the alleviations of her lot, and a welcome sign that, in hastening to the place so strongly indicated to her as the sphere of her future service, she was following the Divine leading.

The committee were glad to be able to act on the recommendations of Bishop Thoburn and Miss Budden, and to appoint Miss Reed to the superintendence of their Asylum for Lepers at Chandag. They had the satisfaction of affording her a suitable sphere of service and at the same time of providing the afflicted inmates with a friend who, while giving them the sympathy and the succour they so specially needed, could also point them to Him who gave it as one of the proofs of His divine mission that the lepers were cleansed.

In penning this record of devoted service among those from whom human nature would instinctively shrink, and remembering that the subject of our narrative is herself most sensitive to suffering, and would naturally be repelled by the victims of this terrible malady, we are reminded of another of God's true saints who made the lepers his special care—St. Francis of Assisi. In Sabatier's account of his life we read:—

"In 1205, just when Francis was struggling towards a full surrender of his will to God, and an entire consecration to the service of humanity, he was one day riding out, and came suddenly face to face with a leper. The frightful malady had always inspired in him an invincible repulsion. He could not control a movement of horror, and by instinct he turned his horse in another direction. He soon reproached himself bitterly. Was the knight of Christ then going to give up his arms? He retraced his steps, and, springing from his horse, gave to the astonished sufferer all the money he had, then kissed the hand of the leper as he would have done that of a priest. This new victory, as he himself saw, marked an era in his spiritual life."

This victory of Francis over the repugnance inspired by this dread disease was not only a notable event in the experience of this holy man, but also the dawning of a brighter day for the lepers of Europe. The brotherhood into which the followers of Francis were organized, following the Christlike example of their founder, made the lepers their special care, visiting regularly the many lazarettos then to be found in England and other European countries. Francis set an example of personal service, often of the most repugnant kind, amongst these sufferers, which the brothers of the order were not slow to follow, and it is probable that from this period the lot of the leper in our land was increasingly alleviated until, happily, the scourge was banished from our shores.

CHAPTER V

AMONG THE LEPERS.

"CHANDAG Heights, the beautiful, in the Himalaya Mountains," is the address from which Miss Reed dates a letter lying before me as I write. It is surely one of the many compensations she is so ready to recognize in her lot, that it is not cast in the sultry slums of an Eastern city, but amidst scenes of natural beauty which are, to her appreciative nature, a source of constant enjoyment. But she shall describe the prospect in her own words:—

"Away to the north, seemingly only two or three days' journey, are the eternal snows whose grandeur and sublimity are indescribable; they are so pure and bright and peace-suggestive! At sunset and sunrise it is easy to imagine them visible foundations of the Eternal City, they are lighted up with such a halo of glory. But it is of the mountains among which I live that I want to tell you. They enclose a lovely valley called Shor, like a massive and exquisitely beautiful frame around a magnificent picture. My home is on the crest of the range which forms the western boundary of the valley, or the left side of the picture frame. And the picture! A rich and beautiful valley, containing about six square miles, lies more than one thousand feet below my lofty and lovely "retreat," and is dotted with numerous villages which are surrounded by clumps of trees and terraced green fields of rice, wheat, and other grains. Through this valley a little river and its tributaries wind in and out, and a ridge of low hills divides it, while almost in its centre, situated on prominent eminences, are the Mission buildings of our Methodist Episcopal Church."

If the feelings awakened among the lepers by the advent of Miss Reed could be recorded, the account would be full of pathetic interest. We know that these sorrowful people were profoundly touched when they understood why and how this new helper had been given to them. Having walked up from Pithora—which was her temporary home pending the preparation of her own bungalow at Chandag—to hold a short service with the lepers, she told them how she had been set apart by God to minister among them. This announcement deeply affected them, and tears coursed down many cheeks as they realized the suffering and self-sacrifice of their new friend. On this occasion, as on others since, they seemed to forget their own affliction in their loving sympathy for hers.

Her own little residence stands on the crest of the hill, some 6,400 feet above the sea level. Eastward it commands a charming view of the valley in which Pithoragarh is situated, while to the West another valley affords a lovely prospect. The gifts of many friends have contributed to make the interior of her home refined, comfortable, and even artistic, and she greatly prizes her "picture gallery," as she terms the extensive collection of photographs with which her rooms are adorned. Music is a joy to her, and an organ, presented by a sympathizing friend, is a source of constant pleasure to one to whom praise is a daily delight.

THREE INDIAN LEPERS.

One of her earliest European visitors, the Rev. G. M. Bulloch (of the London Missionary Society, Almora) affords us an interesting glimpse of Miss Reed in the fulfilment of her ministry of mercy. "We reached Chandag Heights," he writes, "early on Friday morning, and found dear Miss Reed busy in the hospital, tending three patients in a much advanced stage of leprosy. She was binding up, with her own hands, the terrible wounds, and speaking soothing words of comfort to these poor distressed ones. It has always been a trial to her to witness suffering in others, yet she is most devoted in her attentions, and so gentle and kind. We were very much surprised and pleased to find her so active and cheerful, and looking so well. She told us she had never felt better in health, more cheerful in spirits, nor happier in service than she does now." . . . (This is) "not the result of any medical treatment she has adopted, as she gave up all treatment of that sort under a strong sense that God only required of her faith in Him and in His healing power."

Lest any reader should be tempted to regard this as fanaticism or unpractical sentiment, let it be remembered that Miss Reed gladly uses, for her flock, whatever remedies she considers likely to alleviate their sufferings. Her faith is for herself rather than for others in this respect. Moreover, it is doing her the merest justice to say that she is eminently gifted with sound judgment and business ability. The work she has been able to accomplish in less than eight years would not be readily paralleled in the records of missionaries working in the enjoyment of perfect health. Single-handed, or at most with a limited supply of native assistance, she has developed the institution under her charge from a mere collection of huts and stables, in which some 37 lepers were housed, to an establishment with an average of 85 or 90 inmates, sheltered in substantial houses specially erected for them. This has involved the acquisition of at least two considerable additions of land, the surmounting of legal and other difficulties, the arranging of various building contracts, the supervision of native workmen, and the control of the finances as well as the food requirements of her large and growing family. When to these are added the spiritual, moral, and medical supervision of the hopeless and ofttimes helpless beings around her, we have here surely a tale of work and a load of responsibility to tax the strongest. And yet it has been successfully accomplished by *Divine help in answer to daily prayer*, as she herself would be the first to testify.

It is therefore from no feeling of unpractical fanaticism that remedies are dispensed with in her own case, but rather from the deep conviction that even this affliction is in the line of the Divine will for her. As *from* God's hand she received it, so *in* God's hand she leaves it. About this time Miss Reed herself wrote:—

"The disease made most decided progress for six months after my arrival at this mountain retreat, and I suffered intense pain most of the time. But I found His grace sufficient. The everlasting arms are underneath, upholding and keeping me trustful, and I find the love of Jesus adequate consolation, soothing and cheering my heart."

> "There are briers besetting every path,
>   Which call for patient care;
> There is a cross in every lot,
>   And an earnest need for prayer;
> But a lowly heart that leans on Thee,
>   Is happy anywhere."

AMONG THE LEPERS

"Oh, Master, dear! the tiniest work for Thee,
  Finds recompense beyond our highest thought,
  And feeble hands that worked but tremblingly,
  The richest colours in Thy fabric wrought!"

"I am sure His love, His wisdom, and His power are at work. Words are empty to tell of a love like His, He has enabled me to say, not with a *sigh* but with a *song*, 'Thy will be done.' *As God will.* The end may come, and that to-morrow, when He has wrought His will in me."

Quoting from Ruskin, she continues: "In our whole life-melody the music is broken off here and there by 'rests,' and we foolishly think we have come to the end of the tune. God sends a time of forced leisure, a time of sickness and disappointed plans, and makes a sudden pause in the choral hymn of our lives, and we lament that our voices must be silent and our part missing in the music which ever goes up to the ear of the Creator. .... Not without design does God write the music of our lives. Be it ours to learn the tune and not be dismayed at the 'rests.' If we look up, God will beat the time for us."

CHAPTER VI

TRIALS AND TRIUMPHS.

(1894).

THE most definite impression of Miss Reed's life and work among the lepers will be conveyed by quotations from her own letters. For the large number of these placed at my disposal by Mr. and Mrs. Wellesley C. Bailey, I beg to express my sincere thanks. In every instance where it is not otherwise indicated, the extracts from Miss Reed's letters are from her correspondence with Mr. and Mrs. Bailey.

October 9th, 1893. "Blessed be the Lord because He hath *heard* the voice of my supplications . . . My heart trusted in Him and I am helped; therefore my heart greatly rejoiceth."—Psalm xxviii. 6, 7.

"This is a Hindoo holiday, therefore a vacation in the half-dozen schools under my care, and the small army of men who have been working on the boundary-wall, as well as the fifteen or sixteen haymakers, have taken 'a day off.' As I need not therefore give my thoughts and attention to the work of the carpenters and coolies at work on the hospital and men's barracks I hope to be able to satisfy your longing about some of the things I imagine you are wanting to know. . . . Yes, I am more and more satisfied with knowing that each moment of suffering, both mental and physical

TRIALS AND TRIUMPHS

allotted by the dear hand of God, is working out His will in and through this poor, frail instrument. I am comforted that not one unkind thing can be done or said but by His permission. My times are in His hand, *whatever* they may be.

"Two weeks ago I would have said, had I been writing you, that not one was left out of the fold, for to my joy, the last one of the seven unbaptized ones requested baptism, and upon questioning him, I found him much better prepared than I supposed he could have been in the few months' teaching given him. But since that service, two weeks ago, four new patients have been admitted, and we now number fifty-seven—not a great number, but they require much care and prayer, much teaching, training, and nursing. But I am richly rewarded for all I can possibly do for them. In addition to my duties here in the Asylum, I now have six village schools, three Sunday schools, and six pupils in their homes in the village. I am to visit three of the schools every week and the homes every week. In order to reach all the schools, I must ride, walk, and climb steeps a total distance of forty miles, and superintend the teaching of two hundred boys and girls, as well as teach the teachers how to teach. I *enjoy* the work, though it is wearing in addition to all else I find to do."

December 11th, 1893. "Our numbers have not greatly increased this year, only eighty having been enrolled—fifteen of whom have gone away because I could not conscientiously give them leave to go and and come at their own will, nor as often as they wished to visit their relatives. Their relatives visit them quite frequently, and it seems to me decidedly unadvisable to permit them to endanger their friends by remaining for weeks in their own homes. Seven have been baptized on profession of faith in Christ, whom they have learnt to love. Of the fifty-nine now with us, all but six are Christians, and a goodly number of them give clear evidence of a deep experience of God's saving and keeping power. Gentleness, patience, and peace, are now manifest in the lives of some who, one year ago, were unhappy and so quarrelsome that I was often called several times daily to settle differences. Individual care for each one, in addition to the power of the sweet Gospel, adds so much to the brightness and hope it brings into their lives. Human kindness and love seem to make them to realize so much more clearly our Father's love, that my heart is often filled with inexpressible joy because of the tender mercy He has shown me in permitting me, in Jesu's Name, to minister to these my fellow-sufferers. He owns and blesses the lessons taught, and I have some precious meetings in which earnest prayers and intelligent testimony are given. Some have found their way to the Home of Many Mansions, six having died during the year. Truly this has been a year of lengthening of cords and strengthening of stakes of this beautiful retreat, and, during the coming year, I pray and hope that the two new buildings recently completed may be occupied by another fifty of the more than four hundred who are living within a radius of ten miles of us, and who ought to come and share the comforts and blessings so much appreciated by the patients now here. The village and school work I have in addition to my special work here, involves such a large amount of wear and tear that, sometimes, I am very weary, and now is one of those times when I feel worn and hurried.. Pray for me that I may be the better fitted for all the duties and privileges that may come to me with the new year."

On New Year's Day, 1894, we have a glimpse of some of the external difficulties of Miss Reed's work:—

"The villagers are giving trouble about water, and I don't wonder, for I myself think we ought to have a well instead of using water from a stream from which others must drink. There is no water on the premises here, but on the new land there is a good prospect for a good well just inside our wall. I need a wall round the garden and one around my fowl-house, as the jackals, porcupines, and other wild animals, destroy almost all the vegetables, and have carried off more fowls than I use, and I find it difficult to live without vegetables, eggs, and chickens.

On April 4th we hear further as to the water supply:—

"Now about that well. Since writing you I have made a discovery. Finding such a bed of rocks near the proposed site for the well, I feared to risk spending the amount needed to experiment in digging through to the fountain, which I am sure lies under this rocky surface, lest the money thus used be wasted. So I set out upon another search for water, and to my surprise found upon some waste land belonging to Government, a strong spring, within half a mile of our boundary wall. It lies in a deep ravine in an out-of-the-way place, hence my failure to find it before. It sends forth a good volume of excellent water, and by skilful engineering I think the water can be brought around the brow of the hill, conveying it through troughs and ditches into our own grounds. So this very week I am setting men to work to make the troughs and ditches. . . . I am very busy getting ready to leave home this week to attend a great mela at Thall on the Ram-gunga, a river up among the mountains—two days' journey from Shor. I hope to induce a goodly number of my fellow-sufferers to return home with me."

The result of this visit, which was somewhat disappointing, is given in the next letter:—

"For various reasons given by persons of whom I enquired, the mela was not attended by the great throng of worshippers who have been wont to resort to this noted place annually. A native official told me that not one-eighth of the usual number were present. I do not think there were more than 1,000 or 1,200 in all, and among that number I found but four patients who returned with us. My faithful servants made a thorough canvass of the crowds to satisfy my heart that none should be missed. Had we but found and brought in *one*, I should have felt repaid for the journey. There are now just 70 patients in this beautiful retreat at Chandag."

The following extract is from a letter dated August 18th:—

"There are at present 64 patients in the Asylum, of whom 30 are men, 25 women, 7 boys and 2 girls. Of this number 49 are Christians, and 15 non-Christians. There have been but two baptisms this year. I do not urge or ask baptism; when hearts are made new, and the light of the Sun of Righteousness shines in they will ask for this rite. We hear from every direction that the many around us who ought to be here in the Asylum are not willing to come because of the Christian influence exercised. For this reason our numbers are not increasing as rapidly as I hoped they would. I want to spend much of my time in the district, going out to call them in as soon as the rains are over after the middle of September. May I request special prayers for these in the district, that their hearts may be turned to this Refuge, and that all who enter may find Christ as their Saviour, Pray that I may have wisdom, tact, and love according to my need as I go out to urge them to come in. I myself have some weary and most trying days physically now and again, though on the whole my health is a marvel to me. The good hand of the Lord is upon me, and it holds me still, and I trust, and am not afraid of what the future may bring. I am so thankful for the wonderful degree of good health He gives and for the blessed privilege I have of serving Him who is dearer to me than life."

Under date October 27th, Miss Reed speaks of some of the trials of her work :—

". . . experiences some of which would have been heart-breaking did not *He* uphold me, whose I am, and whom I serve. My flock has been the prey of Satan's wiles, and some of my precious ones have followed his leading and gone out into lives of sin. My heart was so rent and torn and I was so weary—not *of*, but *in* the work, which taxes my strength physically—when the way was opened for me to go away for a month for rest and change on a visit with some of my dear old Missionary friends at Naini Tal. . . . I was absent from my post three weeks and a half, travelling over the mountains, camping in my cosy little tent. The visit did me a world of good. Since my return I find the work piled up, waiting for me, and I am busy from dawn to dusk, and my heart is heavily burdened for the souls committed to my care. Oh, please pray for them earnestly, that they may be made free from the bondage of sin."

In a long and interesting letter dated November 3rd, 1894, Miss Reed writes :—

"I began this letter before sunrise, and while sitting at my eastern window writing to you, the sun rose in splendour over the majestic mountains, lighting them up with a halo of glory. The magnificent views I have of the eternal snows and of the beautiful forest-clad heights are a never-ceasing delight to me. Pray for me, please, that my soul's life may be strengthened by the lessons and thoughts suggested by these glorious works of God which lie about me. Did ever mortal woman *need more* the lessons and help to be found in communion with nature and nature's God than this dweller on these heights here, for all around me are not only pain and sorrow, but what is a thousand times worse, *sin*."

This letter contains an account of the moral lapses of some of her inmates which caused Miss Reed much sorrow, and led her to realize the need of more complete separation of the men from the women which has since been carried out. But the year closes with a note of praise for penitents restored. Thus, on December 15th, we find a letter saying:—

"One object I have in writing to-day is the joy of telling you that God is graciously answering my prayers and is pouring out His spirit upon my dear people once more. Humbled, repentant hearts are receiving forgiveness, and being melted into love, and the atmosphere of peace pervading the last meeting we had gave such sweet rest to my tired heart. The Angels, I know, have rejoiced over some of the wanderers who so grieved the dear Lord, but have now "come home" to Him (and to their mother-friend.) Praise His name for ever!!"

CHAPTER VII

PRAISE AND PROGRESS.
(1895).

IN the letters of this year we are not surprised to come upon occasional references to wakeful nights, as well as physical weariness and nervous strain; the matter for wonder is that such references are so few and so casual. The prevailing notes are those of hope and praise, notwithstanding the inevitable difficulties of such a work—difficulties arising through inexperienced assistants and troublesome inmates, together with the labour involved in the extension of the Institution and the daily supervision of the affairs and interests of the little community over which Miss Reed has been called to preside, in addition to her general mission work.

Although the first hurried letter of this year speaks of "the great hinderer" being busy among her afflicted flock, the next is full of thanksgiving:—

"Oh that I knew *how* to express the gratitude my heart *feels* for the prompt responses you always give to my appeals in times of need in the work so dear to you and to me. Words of mine fail to convey my appreciation of the loving-kindness and help so generously and promptly bestowed, and so I console myself with this thought:—'In the grand leisure of eternity we shall have freedom of expression, and then we shall be able to recount the mercies and blessings with which our loving Master crowns our lives here!'"

At a later date, after expressing her concern at the "tiny old mud-houses" in which her faithful servants—("to whom I am much attached")—have to live, we have the following warm expressions of gratitude:—

"I did not expect to have my request granted so soon! That is practical sympathy and co-operation in earnest. The prompt responses you *always* make encourage and strengthen my heart, but never have I been so cheered and rested as by the last two letters, with their enclosures. God is indeed good to me in permitting me to share in this blessed work with you for Him."

On March 16th she writes of that which is ever uppermost in her thoughts, as it is foremost in the objects of the Mission, viz., the conversion of the lepers to Christ:—

"I can only tell you to-day that my heart is filled with joy this week, because of the presence and guidance of Him whose blessing is so manifestly upon the work given us for Him here. A goodly number of the people who came into the Asylum last year are now coming into the fold of our Blessed Redeemer. Some most interesting and precious experiences am I having with them now-a-days. Two baptisms last Sunday, and several to receive the rite to-morrow or next day. Seven or eight more have requested baptism, but I fear all are not fully ready, so I will only present those who appear to be really prepared."

The next letter reports substantial progress as regards the material side of the work. Details are given of the acquisition of five or six acres of land for the erection of new quarters, especially for the male inmates, as well as of the happy provision of an abundant supply of good water for the exclusive use of the Institution—in itself a very great boon.

"You will remember that not *one* spring is to be found on all the land we (formerly) possessed, but now I feel we have all we need; and this building site and location is just what we require. I wish I could write you more fully, but my hand cramps, and I must leave off for to-day. I have great rest and peace in my heart over the whole affair. God's guiding hand and His smile of blessing are so consciously upon all that concerns us here this year that my heart is filled with praise and thanksgiving to Him."

As showing how narrow is the margin between "just enough" and "partial famine" in India, we give the following extract from a letter of June 6th, 1895 :—

"Many, many thanks for your kind letter with first of Exchange received to-day. While I am always grateful for the prompt and generous help you freely give us in this far away Retreat, *this* remittance is doubly precious since a partial famine has raised the price of grain until, now, for one rupee we get only half as much rice and wheat as at this time last year, and it is only with much difficulty we can get any at any price now-a-days. And yet my poor people have never had to go hungry once, while hundreds all about us are suffering from hunger."

To American friends and helpers Miss Reed reports in the following interesting letter, dated April 6th, 1895 :—

"If there be therefore any consolation in Christ, if any comfort of love, if any fellowship of the Spirit . . . . fulfil ye my joy that ye be like-minded, having the same love. Phil. ii., 1, 2.

"To my dear helpers-together by prayer and love:

I have been blessedly conscious, during the past three years, of a fellowship of hearts and an atmosphere of love and prayer surrounding me because of the many prayers ascending from hearts in whom Christ dwells, for this one of His little ones. Many dear brothers and sisters, with whom I have otherwise had no communication, have stood with me; there has, indeed, been to me a deep and real meaning in the words of the text at the head of this letter.

"In answer to prayer, scenes of sadness are changed to those of gladness, and I do not need to *draw* out rejoicings and praise; they just *flow* out. Every token of love from earthly friends is to me a sweet symbol of our Father's love; a pledge of His love to me and to each individual in whose heart He has prompted the desires that find beautiful expression in letters and useful and lovely gifts. For however bright and beautiful the gifts received are, the brightest part is His giving hand. In some ways God seems to be doing for me even more than He promised, not only in supplying my needs, but so many of my 'notions' as well.

"Time is valuable capital to us here. Were my hands, heart, and time not so filled with duties, and did I not have writer's cramp these days, how gladly would I reply to each and all the kind and precious letters received, and thus gratify my longings to acknowledge in private letters the pretty and useful gifts received during the past few months. But my heart is full of loving gratitude for all loving kindnesses, thoughtfulness, and prayers.

"The flowers and garden seeds, nearly half a bushel of them, make these mountain tops and valleys blossom and yield abundant fruit in more than one sense. Tell the dear children I have shared the seeds with at least

PRAISE AND PROGRESS 43

a half-dozen of our native Christian families who live in villages from ten to twenty miles from Pithoragarh. They will bring brightness not only to my poor, dear people here at Chandag Heights, but other mountain tops and valleys are made glad as well. The bandages prepared in such generous quantities are most gratefully utilized, and my poor patients much appreciate the care and comfort given. May I hope for a new supply this year?

" For the comfort of the dear, interested friends who have not read my report for '94, I must add that there is in mission work, as in other things, an ebb and flow of trials and blessings, and the tide turned at the beginning of this year in blessings. Praise Him who is peace, strength, hope, and ' shelter in the time of storm ' for all those who put their trust in Him.

"On New Year's Day my heart was rejoiced by the receipt of a letter from the Society in Great Britain under whose auspices I have been so signally called to work, granting my request for permission and means to purchase more land and erect a branch asylum for our men and boys of the Institution at some distance from the place now occupied by them. Most providentially have I been guided in selecting and buying a beautiful site adjoining our property, fully one-fourth of a mile distant from the house of my women and girls. You see from this that our domain is not a very limited one. I desire you to realize more fully how God has sweetly and lovingly smiled upon us and enabled us to ' lengthen the cords and strengthen the stakes' from year to year.

"This year more is being accomplished than in any of the three years past. In a few weeks seven more new buildings will be completed ; three of these are now in the process of erection, and the other four will be well under way before this letter reaches you. These, when completed, will provide accommodation for eighty people. In the buildings now occupied, seventy-eight are living in comparative comfort, feeling quite at home, and most of them are very grateful for the comforts provided by our dear Lord's good stewards and caretakers.

"Now I must add a few words of assurance to relieve your dear, anxious hearts concerning my health. I would that you could realize how wonderfully well I am. My general health has never been so good as during the past two and a half years. And as for the dread malady which did cause me indescribable suffering until I made my body and the care of my health over to the Great Physician, there are only the faintest traces; the marks have become nearly invisible. They have always been to me like the borings of the ears of the Hebrew servants. (See Ex. xxi. 1 - 6.)

"I will close with extracts from a letter written by dear Miss Budden to my precious mother a few weeks ago; this will help you to realize more fully how well I am. She says:—'I have been up to see your Mary to-day, and we had more than one hearty laugh. I am sure had you been there you would have found more cause for thankfulness than sorrow. The improvement in her condition is nothing short of a miracle; those of us who have known her intimately for the past three years know that for her general health to be what it is, and for all symptoms of this dread malady to be so completely in abeyance that to onlookers they have virtually ceased, show the working of a mighty power in her system that is divine indeed, for none other could accomplish such palpaple results as we witness.'

"The Lord is my strength and my shield; my heart

A GROUP OF LEPERS
Being instructed by the Native Catechist before being...

trusted in Him and I am helped; therefore . . . . with my song will I praise Him."

Referring to a suggestion that some special remedies (Mattei's), should be applied to her inmates, Miss Reed writes:—

"I think it worth while to try them on some special cases. My poor, suffering ones beseech me to find relief for them. My heart aches to see them suffer, and all remedies, tried so far, only alleviate suffering for a short time."

Concerning her own health at this time (in September, 1895), one of her occasional visitors remarked after seeing her, "If Miss Reed had lived in Bible times, and were to show herself to the Priests now, she would surely be pronounced clean. With reference to this, she herself writes:—

"This remark will help you to realize how wonderfully well I have become, and you will rejoice and praise God with me that I am, to all outward appearances, a healed woman! How loving, merciful, and good God is! How gently He has led me! Oh! I have no words to express the tender loving-kindness of His dealings. I will *need all eternity* in which to praise Him."

It should be remembered in this connection that Miss Reed has all along consistently declined the use of remedies in her own case, on the ground that since God had permitted this disease to come to her, she would *trust Him* entirely about it—although quite prepared to apply remedial treatment to her patients.

This neglect of medical agency which arises from absolute subjection to the will of God in her affliction, will not elicit the approval of every reader. But in view of the impenetrable obscurity which still conceals the origin of the disease, of her own mysterious seizure by it, and of the admitted incurability of leprosy, many will not be surprised at Miss Reed's attitude in reference to the use of remedies.

The report of the Leprosy Commission, which made an exhaustive inquiry into the existence and treatment of leprosy in India in 1890-1891, is before me as I write. As the findings of the Commissioners who conducted the investigation in India are in several important points dissented from by the Committee, whose representatives they were, it is difficult to summarize its results. For instance, as to the vital question of the degree in which leprosy is contagious, the Commissioners report:— "That though in a scientific classification of diseases, leprosy must be regarded as contagious and also inoculable, yet the extent to which it is propagated by these means is exceedingly small." From these concluding words the majority of the Executive Committee dissent, and as the names of eight eminent medical authorities are appended to the protest, it may be fairly inferred that the danger of contagion is by no means, so "exceedingly small" as the Commissioners suppose.

But however undetermined this elaborate report of 450 pages is obliged to leave such questions as origin contagion, and heredity in relation to the scourge of leprosy, the Committee and their Commissioners were unanimous on one point, viz., that of *incurability*. By any means as yet known, leprosy, they say, must be declared to be incurable. And this is borne out by detailed returns from upwards of one hundred stations or asylums throughout India. From these reports, we learn that although some 36 supposed remedies were applied, singly and in combination, there is no recorded case of actual cure. " Partial improvement," " slight relief," " temporary benefit," are oft-recurring phrases in these returns, varied not infrequently by such less hopeful terms as "no effect," "no satisfactory result," "no permanent relief," &c.

In view of the mystery surrounding the origin of leprosy, whether considered historically or pathologically; in view of the instinctive repugnance with which it inspires the beholder; in view of its fearful ravages in the human frame, of its incurable character, and, not least, of its place in Holy Writ, it is no far-fetched assumption that regards it as being, above all other forms of disease, a type of sin. Certainly it works in the physical part of man a slow, wasting destruction which bears a close analogy to the evil wrought by sin in his moral nature. How imperceptible in its beginning, how subtle in its working, how relentless in its course, how inflexible in its grasp, and how fatal in its results! How similar alike in its origin, progress, and effects in the body of man is it to spiritual evil in his soul! Should this analogy lead us to wonder how God's providence can be reconciled with such a calamity as has been permitted to overtake one already devoted to His service, we may perhaps find the explanation in the answer of our Lord when asked, "Who did sin, this man or his parents, that he was born blind?" To this enquiry, which expresses the ideas of sin and suffering as cause and effect, the Master made answer, "Neither hath this man sinned nor his parents; *but that the works of God should be made manifest in him.*" And as we read of the boon of bodily relief and of the infinitely higher blessing of spiritual life that have come to many as the results, instrumentally, of Mary Reed's affliction, we must admit that, however inexplicable and painful be the fact of her disease, it has at least led to the *works of God being made manifest in her.*

CHAPTER VIII

A Welcome Visitor

WHILE we cannot too much admire the fortitude and hopefulness, arising from the spring of Divine grace in her heart, which have enabled Miss Reed to minimize the trials of her suffering life and of her isolated lot, yet to ignore the darker side of her experience (as she would have us to do) would be to convey an imperfect impression of her life. Let the reader endeavour to realize the position for a moment. Here is a woman, by nature of a most sensitive habit, instinctively inclined to shrink from physical suffering, especially when of a visible and loathsome kind. Herself mysteriously overtaken by this dread disease whose victims she knows are without hope of human remedy, she is surrounded by a community of doomed beings who are cut off from the rest of mankind, with no longer any share in the hopes and interests of healthy humanity. Think of the burden laid upon her of caring for the souls, as well as for the bodies, of her afflicted flock, of pleading with the indifferent, of reproving the evil-minded, of restoring the backsliding, of cheering the downcast, and of striving to awaken the dormant faculties of these despairing people to the possibilities of spiritual cleansing and newness of life, still, through the Divine love open to them.

A WELCOME VISITOR

And there has to be added to the daily trials of faith and patience inseparable from such a position the bitterest pang of all, viz., the certainty that the same subtle, relentless enemy whose foul handiwork she sees around her at every turn is at work in *herself*, and that she is, apart from a miracle of Divine healing, destined to spend the remainder of her days in separation from those for whose sympathy she most longs, and to whom her affections naturally turn. But let it be borne in mind that this is not *her* conception of her life and work, nor *her* description of the sphere of her labours. This is merely the perspective of the picture as seen from *our* standpoint. To her there is cast over all the dark and repulsive features of the scene a heavenly light which enables her to see in the suffering objects around her possible sons and daughters of the Lord Almighty. Praying without ceasing, labouring without flagging, sympathizing unfailingly, she counts it a privilege to give time and strength, thought and affection, for those with whom her only link is that of a common affliction. Surely nothing but the " love of Christ " could " constrain " to this, and to this she would have us ascribe it wholly. However effectually the fell disease may do its work in that which is corruptible, we cannot fail to behold and to admire the incorruptible beauty of Divine grace in a human soul when, under conditions so adverse, we find a life of such devotion and thankfulness being consummated. Here, beyond question, is the true moral loveliness, " the beauty that endures in the spiritual height."

One of the inevitable trials of Miss Reed's lot, but one which, like the many others, she is enabled to bear with cheerful acquiescence, is its comparative isolation from intercourse with Europeans, and especially with her fellow-missionaries. When from time to time she journeys down from her mountain retreat to Pithora for conference with Miss Budden and others, or pays a visit—a rare event—to her friend, Miss Dr. Sheldon, at her lonely station in Bhot, her heart is lightened by affection and sympathy, and she returns, with strength renewed, to her suffering flock.

At rare intervals she is gladdened by a visit from a sympathetic and congenial Christian friend, such as one of her sister missionaries just named. But one day late in November, 1895, witnessed the arrival at Chandag of a guest long expected and warmly welcomed. Mr. Wellesley C. Bailey, whose own labours amongst the lepers commenced in 1869, was one of the founders (in 1874), and is still the Superintendent, of the Mission to Lepers in India and the East. To Mr. Bailey and his committee was accorded the privilege of appointing Miss Reed to the work to which she felt God had called her, and it was with no ordinary feelings, therefore, that in the course of his last visit to Leper Asylums in India and Burma he approached Miss Reed's mountain home. And no less eagerly, we may be sure, did she anticipate the coming of a visitor to whom her letters, for four years or more, had conveyed many an urgent invitation. I am glad to be able to conclude this chapter with Mr. Bailey's account of his visit, but I may add that the days these two devoted friends of the lepers spent in prayer and communion, social intercourse, and business conference, were full of intense and mutual interest. Some obscure points were cleared up, some perplexing things made plain, sympathy and counsel freely given; the lonely labourer was cheered, and the visitor more than ever impressed as he "saw the grace of God" in the work and in the worker.

A WELCOME VISITOR 51

Mr. Bailey writes as follows:—

"On Friday, 29th November, I spent the whole day at Chandag with Miss Reed, and heard from her all her wonderful story, went over all the place with her, had a little service for the women lepers, and visited the men.

"Sunday, 1st December, was a very happy day, thank God! I preached in Pithora to the native Christians, a good congregation of about three hundred, mostly women. Afterwards went up to Chandag with Miss Budden and Miss Reed (who had been down at Pithora for service and for Sunday School), and after tiffin up there had a most delightful service with the lepers. Spoke on the New Birth. Was greatly helped, and was listened to with breathless attention. I trust there was blessing. After the service, Miss Budden, Miss Reed, and I had singing together.

"To-day (2nd December), spent a very happy day with Miss Reed. Examined D. and N. The former is a very decided case of leprosy which seems to be fast increasing, but N. is, I think, not a leper at all. She has certainly some white spots, but they are in my opinion merely leucoderma.

"4th December, 1895.—Chandag Heights, Pithora. This is Miss Reed's birthday. When I arrived at her house this morning, I found the verandah nicely decorated with ferns and flowers, the work of the Biblewomen and other Christian workers. I spent all yesterday with her, and had a very interesting day. There are some very, very sad cases in this asylum. Poor little Gangali is terribly bad; I did pity her so yesterday when talking to her. She was in great pain with one foot, the toes of which seem literally to be rotting off. She is a little Trojan, and bears her sufferings so bravely.

"This morning, between two and three, Miss Reed was awakened by hearing singing in her verandah, and when she got up and peeped out she found her four Biblewomen and Tima's wife, standing there with lights, singing hymns in honour of her birthday. She is evidently greatly beloved by her workers. The decorations in the verandah were done at night, and Miss Reed knew nothing about them till she got up this morning.

"There is a man here in the asylum whose two children and niece are all lepers, and are here. His wife is the only one not afflicted with the disease. At first only the man and his niece were here. The niece used to live with this man and his wife, and was the first to develop the disease, and the wife and two children, Rupwa (a boy) and Dipah (a girl), were at Miss Budden's home, but after a time the boy became affected, and was removed here, and since that poor little Dipah developed the disease, and has been brought here also. When the poor mother saw that Dipah must go to the asylum too, she was in a terrible state, and said to Miss Budden: 'They have all got it now, and are all at the asylum; I must go there too, I cannot remain here alone.' Poor thing! Miss Budden tried to comfort her, and at last persuaded her to remain where she was, and not risk herself by going to live at the asylum. The disease is developing with terrible rapidity in these two children. The poor boy is scarcely like anything human, and the girl, too, is very bad, though her face is, so far, spared. I believe it was a very, very touching scene when it was discovered that the boy was a leper, and he was removed from the boys' school, where he had been so happy. They are all Christians, thank God!

A WELCOME VISITOR 53

"5th December, 1895.—Chandag, 9.30 a.m. Standing at Miss Reed's door, the sun shining brightly, bees humming, and three exquisite butterflies basking on the flowers of a large bush of heliotrope which grows beside the door, while in front of me and below me the whole of the Pithora valley is hidden from view in one vast sea of white, fleecy clouds, here it is like a genial summer morn in the homeland, down there, under those clouds, is the chill and damp of winter. I am up here to-day holding special services with the lepers. At 10.30 a.m. we all assembled at the side of Miss Reed's house, where the lepers might sit in the sun and be warm; it makes such a difference to them, poor things. At first the women assembled, and Miss Reed had great work getting them all to sit as she wanted them. At last all were arranged to our satisfaction, and the women employed the time singing bhajans till the men should arrive up from Panahgah ("place of refuge"), their home. I stood up, and walked to the brow of the hill to see if there was any sign of the men and boys coming, when a touching sight met my eye. I saw a long, straggling, white line of very helpless creatures wending their way up the mountain-side with considerable difficulty. At last they arrived, and we got them all seated, and ah, what a sight it was! In front of the women, and close to us, were seated three dear little girls with winsome, wee faces, but all far gone in leprosy; they were Minnie, Dipah, and Gangali, all supported by kind friends at home. Amongst the men were several boys with sad, wistful faces—one, a little Nepalese chap, had a specially pathetic look on his face. All were lepers, most of them peculiarly bad and distressing cases. When all were ready we had a hymn and prayer, then I preached to them on an interview with Christ, illustrated by the story of the woman at the well. The Lord opened my mouth, and I spoke to them without any difficulty in Hindustani. It was precious to tell out the riches of redeeming love to such an audience. The appreciative smiles, the nods of satisfaction, and the verbal answers I got from time to time showed that they understood and gladly received what I preached. We afterwards asked those who had really given themselves to Jesus Christ and had received the gift of eternal life from Him to rise. Quite a large number, both of the men and women, did so. I observed the little Nepalese lad hesitating, but finally he, too, stood up. Later on we called together those who had stood up and those who are candidates for baptism, and had a prayer and testimony meeting. Several, both of the men and women, gave the most clear testimony to the blessed salvation they had received through Christ. One young woman, Kaliyani, in a very beautiful prayer, thanked God that He had brought this disease upon her, as it had been the means of leading her to Christ. Amongst our audience to-day were a father, mother, and son, all victims of the terrible disease.

"Sunday, 8th December.—Pithora. A very happy day, thank God. Got my home letters in the morning, then went up to Chandag, where I breakfasted with Miss Reed. After breakfast, service for the lepers in the little chapel, where I had a delightful time. I conducted the service, and preached from "To-day I must abide at Thy house," specially addressing the converts who were about to be baptized. I was greatly helped, and the lepers showed their appreciation of what was said by frequent smiles, nods, and responses. In order to find out how far they understood, I sometimes asked them to finish the sentence, which they

A WELCOME VISITOR

would do correctly. At other times, I would give a wrong turn to something, and ask them if it were so, when they would, without hesitation, correct me.

"There were eighteen baptisms, nine men and nine women. One of the women baptized was Jogiani, of whom Miss Reed had the highest opinion. Jogiani is about twenty-two or twenty-three years of age. She has never been married. Her health has improved since coming to the asylum. Shortly after her baptism, Miss Reed remarked how pleased she looked, and asked her the cause. 'Oh!' she said, 'I feel so happy now, my heart feels so light." She then went on to tell Miss Reed that she wants to visit her old father once more, to tell him all about it. She said she did not expect to do much by singing bhajans. She is no singer, but she could pray for him, and I suppose with him too. She will probably lead him to Christ. One of the Christian women, Kaliyani, such a dear, bright woman, said to Miss Read about the service to-day, 'Oh, I shall never, never forget it!'

"Of the eighty-two inmates now in the asylum, sixty-four are professing Christians. This leaves eighteen still nominal heathen, of whom five are already candidates for baptism.

"One of the newly-baptized women had her first test almost immediately after the baptism. Another woman is very ill, and required someone to sit up with her all night. The sick woman was originally low caste, while this woman who has just been baptized was originally high caste. Miss Reed asked the newly-baptized one if she would sit up with the sick one and look after her. At first she hung her head and did not seem willing, but on Miss Reed putting it to her that she was now a Christian, and all these ideas must go, she consented without any more ado, and so her first stand and fight are over, and she has been given the victory.

"My parting from the lepers was most touching; both men and women assembled to say good-bye, and seemed quite moved. They sent many loving salaams and 'piyars' to all their kind friends at home. The last I said good-bye to were little Minnie and Dipah, who smiled so sweetly and sent their 'bahut bahut,' 'piyar' and 'salaam' to the kind friends who support them. Poor little Gangali was with the women when I said good-bye to them, and I spoke specially to her, and asked her if her foot was better now, and if she were not in such pain now. She seemed pleased at my special notice, and said she was better. Poor, poor child, what a heritage of woe is hers!

"After I left Chandag I could see the lepers watching me for a long way down the road. Once or twice, when I came to a favourable turn of the road, I waved my handkerchief to them."

CHAPTER IX

TRAVAIL OF SOUL.

(1896.)

"O BLESS our God, ye people, and make the voice of His praise to be heard." This is the note of thanksgiving with which Miss Reed opens her first letter for the new year. She had just been cheered by a long-expected visit from Mr. Wellesley C. Bailey recorded in the last chapter, and had also enjoyed a two days' stay in Bhot with her sister-missionary, Dr. Sheldon, who in her turn testified to the help and comfort Miss Reed's presence and counsel had been to her in her lonely post and her difficult work. But probably that which most filled her heart with gratitude at the opening of another year was the fact that during 1895 she had seen as many as 31 of her suffering flock admitted to the fellowship of the Christian Church by baptism. And this out of a number of inmates averaging about 80. Surely the Divine Husbandman has led His handmaiden to labour in a fruitful field! Gratitude for the privilege of successful work is the prevailing tone of the correspondence of all the year. From a letter dated March we take this extract: "Could I but give you an idea of how my time has been filled with happy, blessed work ever since you were here, you would not wonder at my long silence. Aside from my special work among and for my dear people here, I have been called out into the district work in which God has given good success." (In connection with this, it should be remembered that Miss Reed, in addition to her large and trying work among the lepers, was still the missionary of her old Society).

In the next letter we are permitted for a moment to see the veil lifted from the sorrow that has been pressing so heavily on the mother's heart during the years that have elapsed since, all unsuspectingly, she bade a last earthly farewell to the daughter so beloved and to be henceforth so isolated. Mrs. Reed had recently been writing: "My mind has been wandering away to your far-off home. When we do not hear from you every week or two, I cannot help feeling anxious about you. It is now three weeks since we heard. When we hear often, you do not seem so far away. Do write frequently, if only a post-card, so that we may hear from you often, while I stay. . . . Pray that I may be ready when He calls. . . . God is very near to me. He has been good to you and to me." Without intrusion upon a grief so sacred as this, we may surely feel grateful for such a testimony—grateful that she who, of all others, might have yielded to a spirit of murmuring under a stroke so heavy, is found acknowledging God's goodness in so great and mysterious a sorrow.

A touching life-story is recorded in one of Miss Reed's letters, dated April in this year. It is, unhappily, typical of many from amongst India's unnumbered thousands of lepers. "My little girl, Rebli, married when she was eleven years old, and says she lived happily with her husband and mother-in-law for two years, and then the marks of this dread disease appeared on her face. They put her away from them, and gave her a corner in their

A DESTITUTE LEPER IN BOMBAY PRESIDENCY.
(From photo by Mr. T. A. Bailey.)

cow-stable, in which she slept and ate her food, but had to work very hard in the fields the livelong day. She says they were very cruel to her, and that her heart was full of grief because of her affliction. Finally, they tried to drive her away to wander alone in the world, but she refused to go. One day, thirteen months ago, one of my helpers in village work went to this village and was told of this child, and went to see her. He spoke to her of Chandag, and how the people here are cared for, and she came home with him to us. She is very grateful for this refuge, and appreciative of the comforts and care afforded her. To-day, when I told her of the desire of these dear women* (a Bible Class in Birmingham) to support some one in affliction, she said: "Tell them I am so thankful for this home, for I am very happy and comfortable here, and I am so glad I have come to know the Lord, and I do *thank* Him for what He does for me." Rebli became a Christian in less than a year after coming to us, and was baptized in in December last. Her prayers and testimonies in our meetings always make my heart glad. She is a gentle, bright girl, much loved by all her associates. There are many marks on her face, hands, and feet, though she does not *yet* suffer much physical pain, but her poor little heart has suffered, and no doubt the prayers and loving interest of those dear mother-hearts will bring much comfort and blessing to this little one."

Surely the pence, and the prayers, of these good

---

* The cost of supporting a boy or girl is £4, and of an adult leper £5 a year, and any friends wishing to follow the example of these kind working-women in Birmingham are invited to communicate with The Mission to Lepers in India and the East, at 17, Greenhill Place, Edinburgh, Alma, Monkstown, Dublin, or Exeter Hall, London, W.C.

women in busy Birmingham, devoted to the support and comfort of their afflicted little sister in distant Chandag, must be well pleasing to Him who said, " Inasmuch as ye have done it unto one of the least of these . . . ye have done it unto Me."

"A thousand thanks" for a remittance of 1,000 rupees, and gratitude to God that "the rains have set in fifteen days ahead of the usual time," are the burden of a brief note on the 6th of June. " Malaria has even reached lovely and lofty Chandag Heights, and I am having some fever these days, and am obliged to go *slowly, for a change.*"

√ A glimpse of that "travail of soul" which is the mark of the true missionary is given us in a letter of September, when Miss Reed writes, "I am feeling worn and tired the past fortnight, and my heart has been greatly burdened over the souls entrusted to my care . . . I have much to be thankful for; but more over which my heart grieves now-a-days, but I will continue to pray with, and for, these sin-blinded ones, and to try to lead them to Him who alone can cleanse them. Please pray that the Spirit's presence may be manifest in quickening power here. So many need to be quickened and made 'alive unto God' and 'dead indeed unto sin.'"

Part of the suffering by sympathy which she endures is expressed by Miss Reed in a letter of this period. She describes, with deep regret, the desertion of some of the younger members of her flock. Of one youth in particular, whose flight was a sorrowful surprise to her, she says, "I can only account for his running away by the thought that he wanted to see something more of the world than is visible from our beautiful abode here." She deplores the existence of a rendezvous for wandering lepers in the district, where they herd together amid surroundings of the worst kind both physically and morally, and fears her wanderer may have found his way there. (This proved to be the case, but in a few weeks his return is gladly recorded.) But as a contrast, and in some sense a compensation, for this deserter, we hear a cheering account of "Har Singh, a youth of seventeen years of age, who is an inmate of the Institution along with his parents, both of whom are lepers also, and very great sufferers, but "earnest, growing Christians and great comforts" to their kind superintendent. Har Singh, who has been a leper since he was six years old, and is now "a most piteous object," is, notwithstanding his sad condition, a teacher in the school of the Asylum, and has "a good heart, tender and teachable, and has, I trust, received eternal life. His earnest prayers cheer and comfort my heart often, because they tell me he is one who has been made alive by God's Spirit."

One more of these sad but interesting "human documents" may be recorded here from the same long letter: "Gauri Datt is about eighteen years of age. He came to Chandag four years ago with only faint traces of the disease, but had been turned away from home because of these marks, and had wandered begging his food for months before seeking shelter and ease. He was a high caste Brahmin, and doubtless did not wish to come under Christian influence, but when he did come, the truth soon found its way to his heart, and his was one of the brightest, clearest conversions I have witnessed since I have been at Chandag. He has learned to read, and is now able to read his Bible. He has sadly changed in appearance, and his face is greatly disfigured, and he suffers much at times."

In a letter of grateful acknowledgment of some gifts, sent by a London friend, Miss Reed writes:

"Only yesterday I had the pleasure of opening the box you had packed with such loving thoughtfulness. How I wish I knew how to express the gratitude and thanksgiving that filled my heart as I took out the parcels and opened them one by one! The sewing machine is a *beauty!* But of that I shall have more to say after I use it, as I hope to do a few weeks hence in making the 34 warm chaddars (a sort of head covering and wrap combined) for my women and girls for Christmas gifts. Miss Pim has asked me to buy the flannel in India at her expense. Can you imagine the pleasure I shall have in combining your gifts and hers, and my service, to make these poor sufferers happy and comfortable at Christmas?"

The following stanzas from a leaflet much appreciated by Miss Reed may fitly bring this chapter to a close:—

> He who lived this life I'm living,
>   When the robe of flesh He wore,
> Died the death on Calvary, giving
>   Life to me for evermore;
> Risen now and interceding,
>   That His glory I may see,
>   God, my Saviour,
>   "Not a stranger,"
>   Waits in heaven to welcome me.
>
> He, whose constant Presence cheering
>   All my path, my faithful Guide,
> While I wait for His appearing,
>   Longing still unsatisfied,
> Till at length, faith's full fruition,
>   My enraptured soul shall see,
>   God, my Saviour,
>   "Not a stranger,"
>   Will to glory welcome me

Closer than a brother cleaving
  To the soul He died to save ;
Friend Divine ! on Him believing,
  I shall triumph o'er the grave.
He, who bore the shame and sorrow,
  That the victor I might be —
    God, my Saviour,
    " Not a stranger,"
  With a crown shall welcome me.

Blessed Saviour ! closer pressing
  To Thy side my steps shall be,
All my worthlessness confessing,
  All my confidence in Thee.
When amid life's evening shadows,
  Homeward shall my footsteps be,
    God, my Saviour,
    " Not a stranger,"
  Come ! Oh, come to welcome me.

A. F. H.

CHAPTER X

Year by Year.

POSSIBLY a still clearer impression of Miss Reed's work; its nature and progress; its difficulties and encouragements; its light and shade; will be conveyed by extracts from her own reports as Missionary of the W. F. M. S. for a few consecutive years. She writes (February, 1896) :—." Last year I had 5 workers, this year the number has increased to 10, and I am obliged to make tours, at least once a month, camping for a week at a time during these journeys, which take me from 20 to 30 miles from home. But I am glad of these varied duties." The workers here referred to were Hindustani, or native Bible women and teachers, the supervision of whose work formed part of Miss Reed's duties. This will serve to make clear the following extracts :—

" Blessed be God, even the Father of our Lord Jesus Christ, the Father of Mercies, and the God of all comfort.

" Who comforteth us in all our tribulation that we may be able to comfort them which are in any trouble, by the comfort wherewith we ourselves are comforted of God."

" During the past two years I have experienced so much of the loving compassion and tender mercy of 'the Friend that sticketh closer than a brother,' that it is with a very grateful, humble heart I attempt to recount, for the dear friends of our widening missionary circle, something of God's dealings with me and the people to whom He has called me to minister here, in this beautiful place, Chandag Heights. That His seal of blessing is upon the special work going forward among the poor afflicted ones occupying this retreat, as well as among the inhabitants of adjacent villages, will be evident from the following report ;—

"The past two years have been years of improvement —'lengthening of cords, and strengthening of stakes.' The Missionary Society in Great Britain supporting this work, not only sent means for the simple needs of my poor people, but very generously responded to appeals for funds with which to erect the needed additional buildings, so that now we have two large buildings, capable of accommodating sixty men and boys, three smaller buildings for forty women and girls, and a little hospital for separating the extreme cases from less affected ones. To the latter I have a little dispensary attached. Four of these new buildings and a house for a native preacher and family who assist me in village work, have been erected during the past eighteen months.

"The Government recently granted us forty-eight acres additional land, around which we are now having a stone wall built. This generous gift, in addition to the eighteen acres owned by the Mission, provides ample building room for years to come, and allows plots of ground to be portioned out to all who are able to work, while acres are left for grazing ground. So many unknown interested friends have written asking me how this work is supported that I take the liberty of making a brief explanation regarding the Society under whose auspices I have been so mysteriously called to work. It is called the 'Mission to Lepers in India and the East,' and works, not by sending missionaries of its own, but by utilizing existing agencies, making grants of money for the erection of asylums, and undertakes the support of patients who find shelter and care in these home-like retreats.

"Any help from anywhere will be most gratefully received, especially from those who have not hitherto given much to missions. I cannot tell you how sad and how serious the need is here.

"This mountain district, one of the fairest spots of God's beautiful earth, has the sad reputation of being one of the very worst districts in India for this dread malady. During the past eighteen months eighty patients' names have been enrolled on my books, and I am told that within a radius of ten miles of us there are more than four hundred who ought to be here in the asylum. I hope to see the last of these new buildings occupied as soon as the walls become thoroughly dry. How my heart yearns to see all these people, not only sheltered and cared for, but all gathered into the fold of Christ! Of the fifty-seven patients now enrolled, only five are outside the fold. They are new-comers, are being taught, and will, I hope, soon come out of darkness into 'His marvellous light.' The power of the Gospel to bring brightness and hope into their lives has been manifest in the wonderful changes in temperaments which I have rejoiced to note in so many cases this year. I used to be called so often to settle disputes amongst quarrelsome ones, but now peace and gentleness and patience are manifest, and I delight to watch their growth in goodness, and to hear the voice of praise, not in tuneful sounds—(the singing is not good), but in a joyful noise they make unto Him, whom many of them have learned to love. A goodly number give clear evidence of a deep experience of God's saving grace. He owns and blesses the services, and the lessons taught. I have some precious meetings with them, in which earnest prayers and intelligent testimonies make my heart rejoice in Him in whose service there is so much of blessedness. Some have found the way to the home of many mansions.

"Aside from the special work for which I have been called apart. . . I have had the privilege, during the past year, of opening four schools for boys and girls in the villages, lying in the mountain valleys, from two to five miles distant from my home. About six months ago two other schools were made over to me by the preacher-in-charge of Pithoragarh circuit. In these six schools there have been over 200 pupils enrolled this year. They have memorized a number of hymns, texts, and lessons in our catechism, and eagerly look for the Sunday School papers.

"The little boys in the schools are my special adherents, and many a little hand has been the means of conveying the gospel message to idolatrous homes into which I otherwise have had no access, it being a favourite habit of mine to distribute books, papers, gospels, hymns, etc., to all who can read.

"In my attempts to reach the women in their homes, rebuffs and rude speeches have been a frequent experience, and after a whole year of effort I have only five women and one girl learning to read in their homes. I have time to visit and teach them but once a week; but a Bible-woman has recently taken up this village work and gives them one lesson weekly; so with the Bible lessons and teaching given, I trust that such a change may come into their hearts and lives that other homes and hearts will be opened to our visits and to the gospel message the coming year.

"This school and village work involves a large amount of wear and tear, and calls for the exercise of much faith and patience. But I know that it is the steady grind of the work-a-day machinery that in the end produces results which, I trust, shall be better and more enduring than any that can ever appear in a missionary report. My view of progress is a brighter and more hopeful one than even the brightest and most hopeful which statistics furnish.

"It is a wondrous sweetener of what otherwise would be an unbearable burden, that through this dispensation of God's providence and grace He is not only working in my own heart and life to will and to do of His good pleasure; but that it is also being utilized by Him in rousing wills, moving hearts, quickening thought, influencing and enlisting new recruits for the 'great company' needed to publish His blessed word. Blessed, ever blessed be His glorious Name for ever!

"It has been most refreshing to receive the many letters that have come from the dear home helpers, individuals, and auxiliaries, whose precious messages fraught with love and prayer, have cheered and strengthened my heart again and again during the past two years. May I here thank all who have written and who have had no reply to their kindly enquiries, many of which are either answered or implied in this very incomprehensive review, which is so void of details or incidents that I fear it will be wanting in interest to many."?

The Report for the following year reveals to us somewhat of the burden and travail endured by the faithful worker owing to the moral lapses of some who had formerly given good grounds for hope:

"In reviewing the past year's work I am not privileged to reckon up a balance of success. No harvest songs have I to sing—this sower's songs are tears; and to faithfully report the "labour of love," and the trials caused by sins, weakness, and wickedness of some of the flock entrusted to my care, who had been "my joy and crown of rejoicing" until the enemy of souls entered, enticed, and led into paths of sin some of those whom I had thought were settled and established in the faith, is beyond my powers of portrayal. My heart is heavy with sorrow over those who, oh, so much more than comfort need 'to be set at liberty.' Liberty from the *bondage* of sin and Satan. Here, as in Job's time, 'when the sons of God presented themselves before the Lord, Satan came also among them.' (Job i. 6.) Oh! the grief to one who watches for these precious souls as one who must give an account, to learn that some of these called 'sons of God' have not yet really come out from Satan's kingdom into the Kingdom of God's dear Son! How much more than ever before these words, 'to set at liberty them that are bound,' mean to me now! and I am learning from these painful experiences that before broken hearts can be bound up and healed they must first be cleansed. Dear helpers-together-by-prayer, the solemn interests involved here compel me to entreat you, even unto tears, to continue to pray for the salvation of these precious souls, and to pray for me, that in the moments when I most deeply feel my own impotence and the awful force of the 'principalities and powers marshalling their unseen array,' I may hold on to God's promises, and 'lean hard' upon Jesus, who says, 'I know thy labour and thy patience, and how thou canst not bear them which are evil.' May this 'I know' suffice amid all the chilling influences the great Hinderer can put forth this coming year! During the past year eighty-six poor sufferers have been sheltered and cared for. Of that number seven died, four ran away, several had to be sent away for bad conduct, and one case proved that a mistake had been made in the diagnosis, and my heart rejoiced in being able to return one dear girl, healthy and sound, to Miss Budden's school. There are seventy here at present. Leaving all to His patience and forgiveness, and trusting Him to supply all my need of grace, wisdom, patience, gentleness, firmness, and abounding spiritual power, I enter upon another year of service for my blessed Master.

> " He careth, and He will not let
> Me have too much to bear ;
> Nor any burden great or small
> But what He, too, will share.

" No words of mine can express the personal obligation I feel to the dear helpers together across the seas, for the many, many, kind and helpful letters, and for the boxes of bandages, towels, soap, pictures, seeds, etc., all of which have been most thankfully received. Thank you all, very much! and with a very grateful heart I do most truly

> " Thank God for love, the love of friends,
> That golden cord that binds
> Us each to each, and links us on
> To kindred human minds !
>
> That Christlike thing that reaches down
> To depths of human woe,
> And sheds o'er darkest paths and sad
> A benediction glow !

> But thank God most for His great love
>   That living source Divine
> Which stoopeth down to earth, and cares
>   For your love and for mine."

A year later we find the clouds have lifted somewhat:

"Those who read my last year's report will know that it is with no spirit of self-complacency or boasting, but with gratitude and humility, I look back over the year that is now closing, for I recognize that the good hand of the Lord has been upon us.

"At times it has been very heavy, but He has enabled me,

> "Just to leave in His dear Hand
>   All I could not understand.
> Just to let Him take the care
>   Sorely pressing,
> Finding all I let Him bear
>   Changed to blessing.

"We have had a *blessed* year, and that means more than a happy one. And over and above the blessedness vouchsafed, I have had the three essentials of happiness, *i.e.*, plenty of work, remarkably good general health much of the year, and love.

"The care and teaching given to those entrusted to me to serve and train has not been wasted. The work in the surrounding villages has been steadily and systematically done by the four village visitors. Much seed has been sown, and that sown in the nearer villages last year has seemed to spring up and has been cultivated and watered with many prayers this year. And shall we not trust that in due season fruit will appear? For, like a solid rock beneath our feet is our Father's promise that His word shall not return unto Him void, but *shall* accomplish that whereunto He hath sent it. . . . .

"The great event of the year connected with the special work for which I was re-called to dear India, was the purchase of more land and the erection of new homes for the men and boys of the institution. Panahgah (place of refuge) comprises one half-dozen neat stone houses which grew up like magic in a few weeks' time, and this group of white houses is surrounded by garden-plots neatly laid out and carefully cultivated by the dwellers, who are very much pleased with their new abode."

In the following extract Miss Reed gives grateful expression to the value she attaches to the prayers of her many friends, as well as to the stimulus she derives from the "blessed hope" of the coming again of her Lord and Saviour.

"In all their affliction He was afflicted, and THE ANGEL OF HIS PRESENCE SAVED THEM: in His love and in His pity He redeemed them; and He bare them and carried them all the days of old." Is. lxiii., 9.

"August 22nd, 1896.

"Dear Sisters and Friends,

"Greeting and loving-gratitude from a heart filled with praise and thanksgiving to Him who still 'crowneth with loving-kindess and tender mercy' her whom He thus continues to bless in answer to your prayers. He has been so tenderly gracious to me since my last annual letter was written to you just one year ago to-day; it has been such gentle, faithful, 'loving-kindness' all along, and I go on my way sure and glad, taking strength and health as precious gifts from Him Whose presence is salvation. Most marvellously is He fulfilling His gracious word: 'I will do you no hurt.'

"Often and often I am conscious of especial blessing and help given in answer to other prayers than mine. How much the interests of His kingdom, the varied and pressing needs of His work here in this corner of His vineyard need your prayers! Prayer will open the hard hearts of these idolatrous nations, and prayer will bring the little flock for whom Jesus is coming soon. Dear sisters, what can be more majestic than the thought that we, the King of kings' children, have it in our power to hasten the close of the tragedy of sin and sorrow, and to hasten the advent of an era of peace and glory, perhaps, even in our own lifetime. To me it is increasingly precious, the thought that just as soon as the Gospel is published equally to all the peoples of the nations of the earth, so that all may have the opportunity of salvation, and when, from among these, the Bride of Christ be gathered from all tribes and tongues, 'then shall the end come!' (See Matt. xxiv. 14). This 'blessed hope' is a buoy to my soul during the storms and battles that surge round us here, it lifts me above the waves of worry and anxiety.

"Delightful as it is to write to you of our Lord and His dealings with this one of His 'little ones,' I must not take more of your time and mine for this precious theme, because you will be wishing to hear something of the opportunities He is granting to me for service in varied spheres this year.

"I can only give you an outline of the different phases of work for Him in which it is my privilege and joy to be engaged heart and soul.

"Aside from the special work of caring for and teaching the flock of poor suffering ones, which has varied in numbers from 80 to 90 this year, I have been very busy and happy in itinerating and District work, in which are engaged six Evangelists and teachers, besides my six dear Bible women, and in addition to superintending and helping them in this village work, five boys' schools are being opened, and these will be centres of light in needy, neglected corners of this vineyard. . . .

"And now, before closing this letter, I want to assure you that the loving messages your letters bring are real blessings for which I am deeply grateful to you and to Him who puts it into your hearts to send me such cheer and help.

"Yours in His love and service,
"MARY REED."

CHAPTER XI

Christmas with the Lepers

"GLAD tidings of great joy which shall be to *all* the people." This was the message of the angels on the first Christmas morning, and when we find the sad hearts of the lepers of Chandag made happy by Christmas cheer and Christmas gifts, we seem to hear the music of the angelic song still sounding on " through the ringing grooves of change." If the lives of these afflicted and hopeless people can be brightened by the rays of the Star of Bethlehem, then we may be sure that no lot in life is too sad and dark for their cheering and illuminating power.

And that they *can* be so brightened, the following accounts of Christmas among the lepers will abundantly demonstrate.

The Christmas festivities of 1893 are thus described by Miss Reed, in a letter to Miss C. E. Pim, of Dublin, whose interest in the needs of the lepers has been warm and active ever since she helped, 25 years ago, to found the Society of which Miss Reed is now a Missionary.

"I am giving you the tidings of the very happy Christmas I had in seeing all my poor dear people's hearts filled with such real joy and gratitude and surprise over the very substantial manner in which you and your circle of dear workers have manifested the love and care of Him whose birthday had such a joyous celebration in our Retreat here this year. This expression of your loving-kindness has wonderfully helped to emphasize God's love to these, 'the least of His little ones.' These new, bright, warm garments, so lovingly prepared, in His name, for them, deeply touched their hearts; there is an infinite satisfaction to me in the thought that He whom you thus served, heard and appreciated all the salaams and messages I was authorized to send to you! For I cannot *write* them for you, else there would not be space left in this letter to tell you of our Christmas tree.

"I put all the gifts on an evergreen tree which stands near the Hospital: there were dolls for my dear little girls, bright scrap books for the boys, hymn books and other books for all who have learned to read, bags of nuts, etc., oranges in abundance, sweets ($\frac{1}{4}$lb. for each), and last and most appreciated of all, were the warm sulukas and waistcoats; all was a complete surprise to them on Christmas morning. Just after the service, they filed out of our little chapel joyously singing "Jai Prabhu Yisu,"—"Glory or Victory to Jesus," as they went to receive what will make them happy for many weary months to come. Accept my heartfelt gratitude for this help to them and to me, for it is an untold delight to my heart to witness their growth spiritually. Peace, gentleness, patience, and love are being cultivated in hearts comforted and touched through the constraining love being manifested to them in various ways, and I thank you, oh, so much, for your large contribution to this end. I must not write more now. Many, many thanks for the copy of the "Christian Choir." Yes, I have a *musical* soul, and often and often do I prove that *love*, *work*, and *song* cause sorrow to depart. Many of the sweet hymns in this book are very familiar, and I love to sing them in praise to Him who so wonderfully *keeps* and *blesses* me."

Another letter, also to Miss Pim, tells of gifts and gladness in connection with the Christmas of 1895.

"Chandag Heights, February 29th, 1896.—I very much regret my inability to write to you ere this of the happy, blessed Christmas we had here on Chandag Heights.

"The *wondrous love* of Him whose birthday we had such joy in celebrating was made more real by the gifts, the handiwork of those who prepared the splendid warm garments, as tokens of the love of Christ constraining and drawing hearts to thus lovingly minister to the comfort of the "least of His little ones." It gave me more pleasure than I can ever express to present these precious gifts in His name, and I do assure you they were received with loving gratitude, and are much appreciated by all the recipients, who wish to send more salaams than I have time or space to record. But the record of this 'labour of love' is on high. Believe me inexpressibly grateful for the happiness and help you have given to me, and to the dear ones to whom I have been called to minister. . . . .

"The gift of dear Mrs. Buttfield and her husband, affording a bounteous dinner of curry and rice, and cakes fried in ghi, of which Hindustani people are so fond, and sweets and oranges, were 'treats' indeed, which were relished with very *evident* appreciation. How I wish you could have witnessed the scene, the happy, orderly groups, which took us nearly two hours to serve. The services in the Church, too, were greatly blessed, and several received the rite of baptism. . ."

I am glad to be allowed to quote the following graphic account of Christmas, 1896, from the pen of Miss Martha Sheldon, M.D., who is one of Miss Reed's most valued friends. Dr. Sheldon is a Medical Missionary of the Women's Foreign Missionary Society of the Methodist Episcopal Church of America and is labouring in the adjacent territory of Bhot. On several occasions this friend and fellow-worker has cheered Miss Reed by her welcome presence at Chandag, and has, as her letters testify, herself returned to her work encouraged and stimulated by intercourse with her sister-friend. Dr. Sheldon thus describes the Christmas she spent at Chandag:—

"On my way to the Conference from my distant home in Bhot, I was privileged to spend Christmas with dear Miss Reed. In the afternoon of Christmas Eve there was the distribution of warm jackets to the women of the Asylum, which took place on the open grounds; 29 women and 4 girls were already seated on the grass when Miss Reed and I arrived. The sloping rays of the afternoon sun fell gratefully upon us and the poor creatures who sat before us; in the distance stretched the mountains of snow on the North, beyond which lay my field of work among the Bhotiyans and Thibetans.

"After song, talk, and prayers, in which the women took part, the presents were distributed. It was a touching sight to see the stumps of hands, which up to this time had been hidden beneath the enveloping chaddars, now emerge, and in one way or another, appropriate the nice, warm garments which interested friends across the sea had sent, while each expressed her grateful thanks. The girls' presents had been reserved till the last. They received warm chaddars

CHRISTMAS WITH THE LEPERS 79

dainty dolls, &c., &c. As Miss Reed called them to her, and gave them their presents, each girl said, ' Mama, salaam.' Miss Reed turned to me with a smile, and said, 'I have allowed them to call me " Mama " ; they began it themselves—if it is any happiness to them I am willing they should call me so.' "

" In the evening we had dinner together. Miss Reed sitting at her little table with separate dishes, and I at another, eating chicken, curry and rice, and peaches from far away America. We talked with many a ripple of laughter as we enjoyed our meal in the cozy little dining room where the wood fire burned cheerily.

" Then what an evening we had together! There were heart experiences to tell, difficulties of the work to recount, and travail of soul over wayward ones to relate. In the course of conversation, I asked Mary, ' Do you think the disease is making any progress with you?' She said, ' I feel that it will never be any worse for others to bear than it is now, but I am conscious of its presence within, especially during the last few months; but I feel the power of God upon me in holding me quiet. There are days, too, when the external symptoms are aggravated and more noticeable. Then again, they recede. What I pass through in my experience no one knows. The furnace is only heated a little hotter. What dross there must have been in my nature!' she added. ' No, Mary,' said I, ' it is all for the glory of God, and He has honoured you in choosing you to suffer for Him, and to show His keeping power. Not you only, but many, many, are blessed with you.' But I felt deeply that, as far as human help was concerned, she was walking in the furnace *alone*, and that there was only One who could enter in and comfort her.

"Later, at the sweet-toned organ, the gift of kind friends in America, we sang several hymns, including the one beginning, 'Father, whate'er of earthly bliss Thy sovereign will denies,' and the Christmas one, 'Hark the Herald Angels sing.' Then I left to go to my tent which was pitched in her yard. A gentle rain, almost snow, was falling. O blessed rain, greatly needed all over India. It was as though, at this holy Christmas time, the heavens, full of consolation and peace, were gently brooding over a parched and weary world.

"Christmas morning we were up bright and early, as it was to be a full day. After our little breakfast, we went to the dedication of a new chapel which Miss Reed has built at Panahgah, the men's refuge, about a quarter of a mile from her house. As I walked with Miss Reed to the chapel, I realized the exquisite beauty and adaptability of the location. She has, as Mr. Bailey expresses it, 'the whole side of a mountain,' and nature is not niggardly here. Those who are accustomed to look upon Miss Reed's work from a purely sentimental standpoint, do not realize the practical and and permanent character it bears. The Asylum for lepers which, formerly, had been all in one, has now been divided, and new houses for the men and boys built on another and separate portion of the estate. To this locality we went. The rows of neat, well-built houses, with many a green, well-kept garden patch, cultivated by the inmates, presented a pretty sight. The chapel has been built this year. It is commodious and convenient. The caretaker of the men and boys is Yuhanna, a most valued servant; though not afflicted himself, he has, as Miss Reed said, a genuine call for the work.

"Miss Reed's organ had already been carried there, and soon fifty lepers, men and boys in all stages of the disease, were seated on the clean matting in the back part of the chapel. The visitors, including Miss Budden, the preacher in charge, two native pastors and myself, and a number of sweet-voiced singers from the boys' and girls' schools, Pithora, occupied the front part of the chapel. Large, open doors, facing each other, furnished a draught of pure, fresh air between us and the afflicted ones.

"Very touching were the exercises, and very earnest and tender were the prayers that went up to the Lord, who, on this day, made Himself of no reputation, and took upon Him the form of a servant, to serve just such needy ones as these. After these exercises, Miss Reed and I went to distribute the warm, comfortable garments which had come for the men and boys. In giving to these helpless people, or in witnessing the bestowal of gifts upon them, one may enjoy the most unalloyed pleasure of giving. I thought of the givers far away in Great Britain, and wished they might have been present.

"One old man could not wait till he reached his house, but at once slipped his new flannel shirt over his other clothing! Oranges were distributed to all, and an extra dinner of goat's meat and rice provided.

"Miss Reed and I, with full hearts, went back to the house for our Christmas lunch, after which there was a service for the women and girls.

"The sweet memories of this most blessed Christmas Day will ever remain with me."

A few glowing sentences from one of Miss Reed's own letters will aptly close this Christmas chapter. "Yesterday (she writes), we had the *most* blessed of any of the five Christmas Days I have spent in this work and in this much-loved home of His choosing. Never was the meaning of that wonderful word IMMANUEL more consciously realized than during this Christmastide. Surely, surely, the names 'Wonderful, Counsellor, Mighty God, Everlasting Father, Prince of Peace,' given to our blessed Saviour *are* fitting,—

> "Oh! Sing of His mighty love,
> Sing of His mighty love,
>   Mighty to save."

CHAPTER XII

A Vision of the Night.

"FOR God speaketh . . . in a dream, in a vision of the night." Whatever theory the reader may entertain as to the origin and purpose of dreams, the following recital of one will, I think, be found not uninteresting. The lucid account contained in the following letter requires neither introduction nor explanation. I need only premise that it was written by Miss Elise Roper (now Mrs. Buttfield), a friend and helper of the Mission to Lepers, to Miss Pim.

"What place do you think dreams hold in our practical, everyday life? Do they always come as Solomon says, 'through the multitude of business,' or are they sometimes sent to direct our thoughts into a particular channel, or to concentrate them on some special object? Anyhow, I have learned something from dreams, and am going to tell you something about two little visions which have made Miss Reed a personal friend of mine, and the Asylum for Lepers at Pithora a reality it never was to me before. Miss Reed's sad and interesting story lost none of its pathos in the hands of the narrator who told it me one evening the week before last. So the materials for my dreams were prepared for me before going to bed that night. As soon as I fell asleep I thought I was sitting in a room with a bare floor, bare walls, and with little or no furniture in it. One side of the room was entirely open on a verandah, supported at intervals by pillars, between which I looked out, and saw first a white, glaring, sun-dried strip of ground, at one side of which was another building. I could only see a corner from where I sat. Beyond this hot strip, and sloping downward from it, was a green and fertile country, aud beyond that rose mountain peak after mountain peak, in exquisite and majestic beauty. I took this all in at once, while feeling oppressed with an overwhelming conviction that I had a lot of work to do; indeed, I was in one of my inward fusses, knowing that I must get a great deal done, but not knowing in the least what to begin with. I knew I was in Miss Reed's bungalow, and longed to make it snug for her in European style, with carpets, curtains, &c. While fuming over all I had to do and could not begin I became aware of a quiet presence in the room with me. It was a lady seated in a small armchair (the only article of furniture in the room besides the stool I sat on) a little way off from me and near the edge of the verandah. I knew that was Miss Reed, but did not feel the least surprised to find myself in her company. I could only see her profile, but her face seemed pale and thin, with small, delicate features, her hair—dark brown— was parted in the middle, and done in a knot, rather low down on the back of her head. I thought how interesting, quaint, and intellectual she looked, and felt glad she was able to take pleasure in the beautiful view which lay before her. Her right elbow was on the arm of her chair, and she rested her cheek on her right hand as she looked away from me into the distance before her. She was dressed in some sort of an indefinite loose garment, and altogether looked the perfect picture

A VISION OF THE NIGHT

of calmness and repose, while I frizzled all over with an irrepressible longing to go at something or another in the way of work.

"'Miss Reed,' I said, feeling as though I were continuing a conversation began before. 'I want to begin at once, what can I do?' 'Thank you,' said Miss Reed, quietly, 'I really don't think you can do anything just now. I shall soon have everything I want, and am most happy.' 'But look here,' said I, feeling quite exasperated, 'you must let me do something for you. Why, you want everything here, carpets, chairs, curtains. You haven't anything nice about you.' She half turned towards me at this, and seemed rather amused, for she smiled, and then said, 'Oh, you know the Mission to Lepers has given me a grant of fivepence for a muslin curtain, and that really is all I want. I shall put it up there. And she pointed to the space in front of her chair, between it and the open verandah. Here I made a few confused calculations as to how much art muslin it would take to drape the space prettily, and how far the Society's grant of fivepence would go in the purchase of this material. I then began to reflect, also confusedly, on her marvellous contentment, which kept her calm and happy with so much discomfort about her. During these meditations she and the room faded away, then I dropped into a dreamless sleep, or awoke, I am not sure which, but the feeling of longing for scope for my energy went on, and I hated myself for doing nothing. Suddenly I was in the bare room again, and saw Miss Reed standing before me, looking most animated and business-like. Her full face was towards me this time, and now I saw on the right cheek, which before had been turned away, a large, dark-coloured patch, which I felt was the mark of that dreadful disease with which she is afflicted. Beside her was a great tub of water, and she was busy tucking up her skirt preparatory, I thought, to scrubbing the floor. I seized this opportunity for using up some of the energy I was pining to devote to her cause, and, dashing forward, laid hold of the tub with a triumphant feeling of having at last got something to do. But alas! in the moment of triumph, the much-longed-for opportunity slipped from me—the tub refused to be grasped, and I *awoke* with a start to find that my " Mission to Lepers " was as yet unaccomplished, but with a very vivid impression of having had a real interview with Miss Reed. I shall never meet her in the flesh, but from this time forward will ever feel the deepest sympathy with her in the sad affliction God has permitted to come upon her, and also take special interest in her work among the poor lepers of Pithora."

It would appear from the following letter of grateful thanks that this particular dream did not vanish ' like the baseless fabric of a vision and leave not a wrack behind.' Unlike most dreams (either of the day or night), it seems to have resulted in some tangible tokens of interest in Miss Reed and her afflicted flock. Under date of December 20th, 1892, she writes to Miss Roper:

" It would be impossible for me to tell how delighted I was to receive your letter ten days ago, and the beautiful expressions of united love of the little circle who prepared the petty 'trifles,' as you call them, contained in the box, which received a welcome last evening. Each of you must have been greatly blessed indeed by Him, ' who is not unrighteous to forget your labour of love which you have shown towards His name,' for has He not told us, ' It is more blessed to give than to receive.' And since the expressions of your kindly thoughts and wishes have been such a blessing to my heart, how greatly, I say, you must have been blessed in giving. These precious gifts are more highly valued because I am sure our loving Heavenly Father prompted you to this kind act, and so I give a grateful and cordial welcome to the love which designed and prepared these memorials—and they are all *so beautiful*, too, as well as useful. I do admire the selection of these delicate colours, and am *so* pleased with all the articles, each of which is most acceptable. This beautiful art muslin will be useful in draping *two* doors, instead of only the *one* you saw in your dream. (How very strange that you should dream about my little home.) One door leads from my little sitting-room into the east verandah, and the other into the verandah facing the west. I had no drapery for either. These beautiful mottos are inscribed with precious texts which have so often comforted and cheered my heart. Over and over again, during the past two years, have I sung this favourite hymn (a copy of which I enclose)* which has so voiced my experience, that it has become peculiarly

> *" My times are in Thy hand,"
> My God, I wish them there ;
> My life, my friends, my soul, I leave
> Entirely to Thy care
>
> " My times are in Thy hand,"
> Whatever they may be ;
> Pleasing or painful, dark or bright,
> As best may seem to Thee.
>
> " My times are in Thy hand ;"
> Why should I doubt or fear
> My Father's hand will never cause
> His child a needless tear.

> "My times are in Thy hand,"
> Jesus, the crucified !
> The hand my cruel sins had pierced
> Is now my guard and guide.
>
> "My times are in Thy hand ;"
> I'll always trust in Thee ;
> And, after death, at Thy right hand
> I shall forever be.

sweet, since *He* has enabled me to trustfully say, and to sing from the depths of my heart, 'My times are in Thy hand.' I find so much help and blessing in song, and from day to day, I *prove* that '*faith, hope, love, work* and *song*, cause sorrow to depart.' Oh, how my heart goes out in praise and gratitude to Him who so wonderfully verifies His blessed promise, 'Lo, I am with you alway.' With me, not only keeping and blessing my own soul, but He has condescended to use me, a poor, weak instrument, in blessing others. Blessed, ever blessed be His Name! So many precious testimonies come to me through scores of letters received from known and unknown friends, telling me that our Father is graciously using the affliction He permits to come on me in touching hundreds of hearts, leading them to a deeper, fuller consecration to His service, of time, strength, means, and heart. The joy of being thus used for the advancement of His Kingdom is, to me, a richer feast than millions of those who enjoy health and all earth's comforts can ever know. What infinite comfort and blessing in the blessed assurance that a wise and loving *purpose* underlies the mysterious providence which calls me to this *special* service for Christ.

"I presume that dear Mr. and Mrs. Bailey keep Miss

Pim (our Hon. Sec.) informed about the growth of all the interests connected with this mission work, both here and elsewhere. I endeavour to write very frequently and very fully from this outpost, that they may be enabled to make real to all who are interested in the Mission the needs of my fellow-sufferers—no, I must not say fellow-sufferers, for though *they do* suffer so much, the great Physician has *my case* in hand, and so wonderfully hears and answers the believing, importunate prayers from multitudes of hearts being offered for me, that He wards off the pain, except now and again when He lets me know what *they* endure; but my heart suffers more with them than I could ever do, should this dread disease be allowed to run its course in this 'house of clay.' So, in *that* sense, I am a fellow-sufferer, and oh! how thankful am I, how humbly and devoutly thankful, that (I say it with reverence) He *does* use me in binding up the broken-hearted—to give unto them 'beauty for ashes, the oil of joy for mourning, the garment of praise for the spirit of heaviness, that they might be called trees of righteousness, the planting of the Lord, that He might be glorified.'

"My letter is growing too long, but I would like to tell you before closing that my precious mother's heart will be much touched by your loving-kindness. I shall send her your letter, and a description of each article your box contained, for no pleasure is complete for me unless, so far as it is possible, it is shared with her. And then, too, when I tell you that her mother was born at Strabane, in the North of Ireland (her maiden name, grandmama's, was Anderson), do you not imagine her heart will be touched by the mementoes coming from the land of her mother's birthplace?

"Now, with more gratitude than words can express, to each of the dear sisters whose names you mentioned, and whom I shall love to think of as praying for this work so dear to my heart, and trusting that you will pray that I may have the abiding presence of the Holy Spirit, that I may be strengthened with all might according to His glorious power, unto all patience and long-suffering with joyfulness.

"Believe me,
"Yours very gratefully,
"Mary Reed."

CHAPTER XI

Divided Duties

(1897.)

THOSE who have so far followed this record of steadfast service under conditions of exceptional difficulty will not be surprised to find the strain beginning to tell, as Miss Reed herself expresses it, on " my health as well as on my heart." For upwards of five years, with few and brief intervals of rest, she had been fulfilling a two-fold ministry. Not only was she district missionary for the Women's Foreign Missionary Society, but also Superintendent of the large and growing Institution for Lepers. In the former capacity there devolved upon her the supervision of a band of native Bible-women, whose labours extended over a wide area, as well as much direct spiritual and educational effort, while, in the work to which she has been so specially called and consecrated, many duties, both painful and exhausting, had to be personally performed.

Let us review the situation briefly: Pressed by the varied duties arising from the two departments of work just noted; dependent solely on very limited native help, in frequent contact with suffering and death in its most loathsome form, and painfully reminded from time to time of the presence of this most dreaded malady in her own person—no surprise need be felt that the strong brave spirit seems to falter for a moment, and that occasionally the entries in the diary for this year sound a despondent note.

I am glad to be permitted to reproduce some extracts from Miss Reed's daily journal for the early months of 1897:—

January 1st.—" Praise God from whom all blessings flow," was the first thought that entered my mind as I awoke at dawn on this New Year's morning; and then followed the precious promise " Certainly I will be with Thee." May my heart and life praise Him continually throughout the year! I sat down at my organ and played and sang—

> Come, let us anew our journey pursue.
> . . . . . .
> His adorable will let us gladly fulfil,
>   And our talents improve,
> By the patience of hope and the labour of love.

January 3rd (Sunday).—No message from above this morning when I awoke. Sick and in pain almost all day. Misery indescribable. Very stupid and dull, too. However, I managed to teach the Sunday School lesson to my women and girls.

January 4th.—No message this morning after a wakeful night. Worked at accounts and wrote letters to-day. Taught women and girls from Hebrews, chapters ix and x, and had a good meeting.

January 10th (Sunday).—Most trying day of physical suffering. Much depressed mentally, and not bright and happy spiritually.

January 12th.—Much better to-day. Lessons given

THREE BURMESE LEPERS.
The one with the gong is a converted Buddhist monk.

and letters written in the morning. Spent the afternoon with Miss Budden.

January 24th.—A blessed meeting with the women to-day, lesson from Ephesians, chapter iii.

January 25th.—Went to Panahgah (the quarters for the male lepers), but was not able to give the Bible-lesson. My throat too painful to talk to-day.

April 12th.—A glorious day! My heart rejoices with joy unspeakable over Tarwa's *conversion*. His face is *so* bright and his heart *so* happy, it delights my soul to look at him. The Sunday School lesson yesterday, "The Conversion of Cornelius," affected him deeply, and after an almost sleepless night—spent in prayer, he says—he was converted in the early morning in his little room at Chandag. Now that he *knows* Christ's power to save, and to forgive sins, may he know also His power to *keep* and be eternally saved!

April 24th.—A glorious victory Tarwa won to-day through the grace and strength that Jesus gave him. We had a solemn time with his mother and brother, and finally they yielded for him to be freed from performing the idolatrous ceremony on the anniversary of his father's death to-morrow.

April 25th.—A blessed day. I went down to Pithora to hear Mr. —— preach, and was so delighted to meet Tarwa and his brother with their faces towards Chandag, on their way from Sunday School, instead of going home to-day. They knew the Brahmin priest was coming to perform the ceremony of their father's sharád. They were absent, and thus Satan was foiled. They are by this brave act set free from idolatry. May the Son make them "free indeed!"

These earlier entries give us a glimpse of the times of bodily suffering and mental weariness, which have been so minimized by Miss Reed in the many letters used in the preparation of this biography. It is well that the veil should be so far lifted, in order that the sympathy to which she is entitled, and the prayers she so much values should be called forth. These selections from Miss Reed's diary may be supplemented by the following record of one day's duties—a specimen doubtless of many—(Wednesday, October 5th):—

" Immediately after chota hazri went to the Hospital and spent more than an hour giving directions and seeing them carried out, about the making of the concrete floors.

" Called and examined my class of six boys in Hindi 1st book. They are making good progress for boys who suffer so much—poor fellows! I hope they will be ready by Christmas to read the Testament intelligently.

" Next, a call from some villagers, pleading for a school for their village.

" Settled down with account-books, on camp-stool in verandah of Hospital, so as to oversee the workmen and do accounts. An hour spent thus.

" Call from native preacher in charge of Pithora, who called for my report of the schools for his annual report.

" Another hour given to carpenters and accounts. Home to breakfast at 12 o'clock.

" After breakfast called a woman, one of my helpers, herself a sufferer; gave her carbolic soap and directions for bathing and dressing wounds of a new case, recently admitted. Gave out clothing for another new woman.

" Went to look after people cutting grass and making hay. Returned home, swept and dusted, and set my house in order. Transplanted some pansies.

" Had lunch, and then called to see Miss Sheldon.* Called to see the cook's son, and gave him some medicine. Spent another hour with carpenters. Then, a wild-goose chase to see a lame woman, who sent word pleading for admittance to the Asylum. *Not* a leper, only wanted food and clothing. Not admitted.

" Rang the bell to assemble people for service. Gave lesson, and then at sunset walked down the hill half a mile and back.

" I trudged up the hill, stopping to see Dr. S., then came home to dinner, read for an hour or so, and finally scribbled these notes of my day's work."

It is gratifying to note how the lives of the lepers are brightened and their characters improved by their experiences in the Asylum. Evidence of this is afforded us in a letter giving some particulars for the information of those who have kindly become responsible for the support of individual inmates. Respecting some of these Miss Reed writes :—

"*Chandra,* a woman of 30 years or upwards, is growing in usefulness, and during the past year has become one of my three matrons. She has the oversight and care of six or seven women and girls, to whom she is learning to minister help. She used to be a most selfish mortal, and the joy of service is a new one to her. Strange to say, she is more healthy now that her soul-life has begun to prosper.

"*Parli* is a girl of about 17, who has been here only five months, but has improved wonderfully in that time, just by being an attentive listener while our Christians were being taught their little catechism. She learned to repeat the whole of this with only one slight

* Dr. Sheldon was on one of her occasional visits to the neighbourhood, from her station in Bhot.

mistake. Her heart seems permeated with the blessed influence in the lives of Kaliyani, and her own sister Rebli, and others who take delight in teaching her of Christ. She would receive baptism to-morrow if permitted to do so, but I cannot consent to it until she experiences an outright change of heart. I shall, however, pray and look for her conversion. She is learning to read, and was so happy two or three days ago, when I told her I would ask special prayer for her (This prayer was answered, and on August 13th Parli joyfully confessed Christ in baptism).

"*Kaliyani* is a real deaconess in her works of love, untiring in her ministry, and manifesting the sweet spirit of the Master. She is a blessing to all and a great joy and comfort to *me*. She is very happy that you have enrolled her trying brother Nankiya in your list to be prayed for. Verily a change does seem to be coming over him. He has suffered much lately, his feet have been in a terrible condition. He, too, is reading the New Testament daily with a teacher.

"*Dipah*, poor little girl, has become more of a sufferer, and it makes my heart ache to witness her sufferings—such a gentle little thing she is. The disease makes much progress in her little brother Rupwa. He is much disfigured and is hard of hearing.

"*Gauri Datt* is growing in knowledge and years and is a great comfort to Yuhanna, because he is developing into a most earnest Christian. The disease makes much progress in his case.

"*Har Singh* has become a teacher of the men and boys who read and of those who are learning. He goes down to Panahgah from his home here (his parents are at Chandag) four times during the week to teach his classes. His father and mother suffer terribly and almost constantly. Har Singh repeated the Catechism from beginning to end to me this week without one single mistake. I do not teach this by rote either, but ask many questions, bringing out all the many good points in this excellent little book."

These notes of special cases may be supplemented by an extract in which Miss Reed speaks of the effect of her work on the lives of her inmates in more general terms.

"As to the spiritual life among my dear people at Chandag Heights, I am deeply gratified to be able to say my heart is often made happy by evidences that *other* hearts have been made new. The Holy Spirit's blessed influence permeates, teaches, and enlightens minds, and comforts hearts that used to be filled with only thoughts of self seemingly."

Chandra tasting the joy of unselfish service; Parli drinking in the Divine teaching, influenced by the lives of others; Kaliyani showing the Spirit of Christ in her steadfast service; little Dipah bearing her terrible sufferings with gentle submission; Gauri Datt growing in the spiritual life; Har Singh gladly teaching his fellow sufferers; as well as the fruit of the spirit manifested in many others; these are cheering points of light, as they shine out from the dense darkness of heathen ignorance and of foul disease. Let it be remembered that these are they that are counted unclean or outcast by all save the Christian Missionary, and that, apart from such beneficent work as that of Mary Reed, they would almost certainly be enduring the wretched lot of the homeless leper. This surely is to find the jewel in the mud, and to cause the desert to blossom as the rose.

As the question of Miss Reed's health, and the progress or otherwise of the disease in her own case, is to many, of equal interest with the story of her work, quotations from two letters of 1897 are appended, which reveal some of her experiences in this respect. In touching on this subject, I wish as far as may be, to imitate the reticence which characterises all her own references to it. An obvious shrinking from the use of the words "leper" and "leprosy," together with a brave determination to make the very least of her symptoms and sufferings, give added weight to the mildly expressed allusions to be found in Miss Reed's letters, and of which the following are specimens:—

February 6th, 1897.—"I, myself, am not in the best of health. I have some very trying sieges, though there is no cause for anxiety. I am *kept* through all . . . The 'Friend that sticketh closer than a brother' is so tender, and His presence *is* salvation from sin and from care. His love satisfieth."

Towards the close of this year the shadow of suffering seems to be falling more darkly over her life. In November she writes:—"My throat is becoming much affected by disease, and is often very painful, and I feel as if I could not talk and sing more than I do in my work among my own people, during the coming year. I am becoming a fellow sufferer, with many of them. Their throats cause them much pain. A certain type of the disease has affected a dozen or more of those now here. Some have lost their voices entirely, and suffer agony at times to get breath. They are all praying much for me lately, and dread to see me suffer. I am alone this month, as Yuhanna has gone to Naini Tal to attend District Conference. I miss his help much. I go to Panahgah to have service with the men and boys every day and to minister to the sick ones, of whom there are a goodly number who are in an indescribable condition just now."

A very pleasant experience may find a record at this point. In May of the year under review Miss Reed had the great enjoyment of meeting her co-workers of the Women's Foreign Missionary Society at their Sanatorium in the hills above Almora. Thither, at their cordial invitation, she journeyed for fifty miles, camping in her little Swiss-cottage tent, which also formed her dwelling during her sojourn with her friends. It was pitched in the shade of an evergreen tree in the lovely grounds of the Institution, and beautified by her sister missionaries with flowers and shrubs and creeping plants.

The gracious act of these friends in welcoming her into their midst once more was much appreciated by Miss Reed. Not only for her own sake did she value it, but also for the assurance it would give to her dear home circle that the disease was being kept in check, and had not as yet developed to such a degree as to render her an absolute exile.

If the Lord of the harvest has specially fitted His servant by painful experience to labour in this difficult work, it is that she may reap many golden sheaves from a field which, to human eye, would appear so unpromising and uninviting. At the close of 1897, we find eighty-five lepers being sheltered and cared for in the Asylum, of whom sixty-seven had confessed their faith in Christ by baptism, and in many of whose lives the fruit of the Spirit was being manifested. This large proportion of conversions testifies powerfully to the fruitful character of Christian work among this afflicted class. The outcast leper is pre-eminently ready for the Gospel of Christ. With no help from his kindred, no hope from his religion, no remedy for his disease, no means of subsistence, he is surely, of all men, most miserable. When to people in such a plight as this the Christian Asylum offers freely food, clothing, and shelter, as well as bodily relief and spiritual hope, small wonder that the lepers are found pressing into the Kingdom. It may well be questioned whether any form of missionary and philanthropic effort better repays the self-sacrificing labour and the money expended upon it than this work of caring for the bodies and souls of God's lepers.

CHAPTER XIV

Light and Shade

(1898.)

THE Autumn of 1897 found Miss Reed so weary and worn physically that she was at length obliged to seek relief from further service as a missionary of the American Society, whose representative she had been since her arrival in India in 1884. The severe demands of her special work among the lepers, together with the subtle inroads of disease, had at length made this step imperative. The final severance of official relations with her old Society did not, however, take place till October, 1898, at which date Miss Reed entered upon undivided service for the Mission to Lepers in India and the East. The committee gratefully recognized the valuable service she had already rendered them, and thankfully accepted her offer of *entire* devotion to their special work. When it is borne in mind that the management of this large institution devolved upon Miss Reed, assisted only by one caretaker and one servant, both natives, it will be recognized that work, more than enough for the strongest, lay ready to her hand. The supply of sufficient and suitable food, the simple, but very necessary, medical treatment, the directly religious work, comprising many services, classes, and meetings for prayer, the correspondence and bookkeeping, the general supervision—all these, *plus* the incessant incidental claims upon time, strength, and sympathy, surely demand an expenditure of physical and spiritual energy which can only be made good by "the supply of the Spirit of Jesus Christ," and by a constant waiting upon God for the renewal of daily strength.

In a letter to the headquarters of her Society in America, Miss Reed says: " I must be free after October 10th, 1898, from the very unsatisfactory effort I have been making for nearly seven years to serve in two capacities. . . . From my childhood I could never do things by halves, and have a satisfied heart and mind, and as the years have passed since I came to these Heights I have found the effort to do two things, *i.e.*, serve under the auspices of two Societies, increasingly difficult. And now that disease—though so slightly manifest outwardly, thank God for His tender mercy— affects my throat more and more, and preys upon my system, I do not feel equal, physically or mentally, to try longer to serve in two capacities. And, whereas I have recently been adopted by the entire Committee of the Mission to Lepers . . . I trust you will give me leave to reply that this change may take place on October 1st, 1898. I fix that date in order to complete my fourteen years in connection with the W.F.M. Society, I shall ever continue, as I have time and strength given, over and above that needed for the special service for which I have been "set apart," to help, when and where I can, in this end of the earth—so full of opportunities to proclaim salvation, full and free, through Jesus Christ our Lord."

Very brief quotations from the replies of the two Secretaries of the American Society will suffice to show that the facts of the case were recognized by them, and that they regarded Miss Reed's request as a reasonable one.

Mrs. Cowen writes in terms of warm appreciation and continues, "I am glad you have given up, or will give up, your double work. It has been too much for any woman to do and do justice to herself, even if she had good health."

Mrs. Stevens says: "I am confident that the work of the Mission (to Lepers) is all you can do without overburdening yourself, and we would not have you do that."

These frank and kindly assurances enabled Miss Reed to enter hopefully on the closing period of her dual service, during which time considerable itinerating work was accomplished in the regions lying around the Shor district, among the many villages of which Miss Reed had now for seven years gone teaching and preaching Jesus Christ, and whence doubtless fruit of her efforts will be seen in the day when every labourer's work shall be made manifest.

From an interesting letter, dated June 16th, 1898, we take the following extract:—

"This is an exquisitely beautiful morning—clouds and sunshine chase each other over the mountains, hills, and valleys that lie within my range of vision. There is a break in the rains to-day—the monsoon set in up here in May this year, a whole month earlier than usual. I have brought my writing materials, with chair and table, into the front (east) verandah to get the benefit of the delicious atmosphere and to enjoy the beauty of the fleecy, flitting clouds, and the smiling landscape, of which I have a magnificent view from my lofty and lovely abiding place.

" As I have been writing to you, and looking out now and again upon the beautiful scene before me, I have recalled to mind a gem from Ruskin, he who so loves the true, the beautiful, and the good. I must share it with you—so here it is, an extract from one of my treasures :—' There is not a moment in any day of our lives when Nature is not producing scene after scene, picture after picture, glory after glory, and working still upon such exquisite and constant principles of the most perfect beauty, that it is quite certain that it is all done for us and intended for our perpetual pleasure. The sky is fitted, in all its functions, for the perpetual comfort and exalting of the heart; for soothing it, and purifying it from its dross and dust. Sometimes gentle, sometimes capricious, sometimes awful; almost human in its passions, almost spiritual in its tenderness, almost Divine in its infinity, its appeal to what is immortal in us is as distinct as its ministry of chastisement or of blessing to what is mortal is essential.' "

But when we turn from the lovely and suggestive scenes of nature in some of her sublimest aspects, to the effects of sin and disease on what should be the noblest part of God's creation, sad reflections await us. In this same letter we read of an event which (and not for the first time) deeply grieved the heart of this friend of the friendless. This was the flight from the sheltering, though at the same time restraining, care of the Asylum, of two couples who broke away, there is too much cause to fear, to a life of sin. Since separate quarters had been provided for the male inmates at Panahgah, in 1895, Miss Reed had been spared this particular form of trouble. Being both missionary and mother to her flock, such a trial as this would in any case have been keenly felt, but it derived an added pang from the

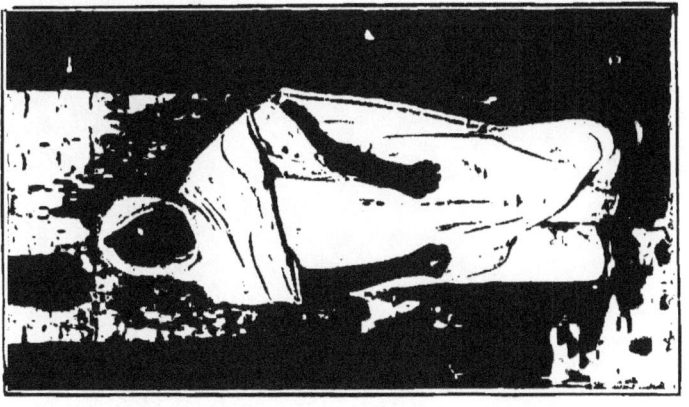

A LEPER WOMAN
(In the Purulia Asylum.)

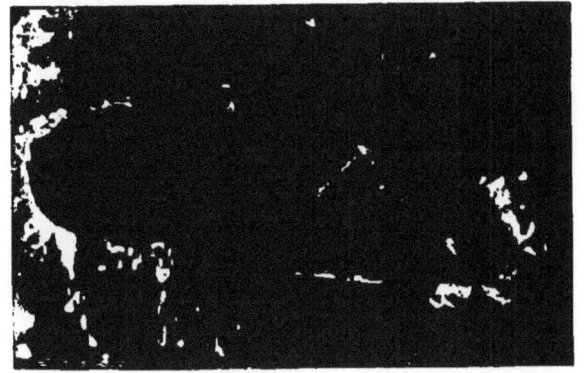

A HOMELESS INDIAN LEPER.

circumstance that one of the runaways was a young girl, only 13 years of age, of whom Miss Reed had made a special companion, and for whom she felt a special affection. While she could be kept in close association with her benefactress this poor child was safe and happy, but the disease had in time so disfigured her that her transfer to the women's quarters was absolutely necessary. Here she fell under the evil influence of a wicked and hypocritical woman, who finally induced three others to accompany her in her flight. (It may be added that this girl and her companion, a young man of 18, have both since returned with professions, apparently sincere, of penitence and regret).

Such an incident need occasion no surprise, and should certainly suggest no question as to the kind supervision exercised in this or in any of the Asylums of the Mission to Lepers. The inevitable restraint and mild discipline of institutional life form a contrast to the unbridled license of the homeless leper's wandering existence. Herding together in encampments or colonies, these outcasts from the common life are exempt alike from moral influence and legal supervision. In thousands and thousands of cases the one thing the authorities do for these miserable people is—to leave them alone! Losing by their leprosy almost all that makes life dear, they gain liberty, at least, and who can wonder that liberty with them means license to live as they list—a law unto themselves? Gathered in, in most cases, from an existence of aimless wandering and unbridled restraint, it speaks eloquently of the kindness and comfort they meet with in the Asylums that instances of flight are so rare. The following testimony, given recently by His Honour the Lieutenant Governor of Bengal, respecting the Society's large asylum at Purulia may be quoted here, as it would apply with equal force to the institution under Miss Reed's care: "I have been greatly impressed by my visit to this asylum. It has now upwards of 500 inmates, and the sight of so great a company of stricken people would have been most distressing had it not been for the surprising contentment of their bearing. No leper is sent by the authorities, and no wall prevents an inmate from leaving, and yet the numbers rapidly grow—evidence of the constant kindness and sympathy with which the poor creatures are treated. I have seen no more truly benevolent work in India than this."

The question of occupation and medical treatment are of great importance in connection with work among lepers. Any form of work, or even of pastime, which relieves the tedium of their weary days and gives them the sense of being useful is helpful to them, acting, as it does, as a kind of mental tonic. But it is only in the earlier stages of the malady that they are capable of even the simplest forms of labour. Writing of some of her less afflicted inmates, Miss Reed says: " Every day, from 9 o'clock to 4 or 5 p.m., they graze the cows. I arranged this that they might be kept in the pure air, and as much as possible away from those in whom the disease has made more headway. I give them in the first stages medicine three times a day, to arrest further progress as long as it may be possible. They are all improving so nicely. There is now not one mark on Punnia, except a faint reddish tinge occasionally on her cheeks where there were marks when first the disease appeared." Gardening is both a pleasant and useful form of occupation for those less affected, who are also encouraged to do all in their power for others who have become practically helpless. At the close of 1898 Miss Reed reports twenty inmates as either able to read or learning to do so, nearly half of this number having learned since their admission. Two interesting and encouraging Bible classes were also being conducted by Miss Reed—one at Chandag Heights for the women and girls, and one at Panahgah for the men and boys. In addition to these classes and other services, the children in the little community were being taught to read, and were learning to be helpful to others.

Of the seventy-nine inmates at the end of the year, fifty-five were Christians and twenty-four non-Christians. Nine died during the twelve months, of whom six gave good evidence that they passed away in the faith of Christ and in hope of a perfect life hereafter. Among the new admissions were two girls,—one from distant Meerut, and the other from Bareilly—the latter from a Girls' Boarding School in connection with the Methodist Episcopal Mission.

CHAPTER XV

The Prayer of Faith

(1899)

THE most notable event in Miss Reed's experience of this year was her visit to Lucknow in January and February. She journeyed thither at the unanimous request of the Missionaries of the Women's Foreign Missionary Society (of America), with whom she had been so long associated, and who, at their North India Conference in 1898, had passed the following resolution:—" That, as year by year, we hear that our sister, Mary Reed, is not only continuing in active service, but is also in better general health than in former years, we assure her of our sincere gratitude to God for His great goodness to her, and of our prayers that He will bless all her service in His name, and we send her a hearty invitation to attend our Annual Conference (of January, 1899), and to give us the joy of welcoming her in our midst once more."

In accordance with this invitation, Miss Reed packed up her camp outfit and made the eight days' journey to the foot of the mountains, in the congenial company of her dear friend, and sister-missionary, Dr. Sheldon. From Kathgodam, 18 or 20 hours by rail brought them to Lucknow, where a right royal welcome was accorded to her who had been for nine years absent from the

THE PRAYER OF FAITH

gatherings of her colleagues. Profound gratitude was the uppermost feeling in Miss Reed's mind, at finding herself once more assembled with so many friends and fellow-workers, and when Bishop Thoburn summoned her to the front with a request that she should address the audience, she felt unable to utter any words but those of praise. As she stood before that great company, the desire was flashed into her mind to express her thanksgiving in song. She simply said, " ham git gâwen " (let us sing); and joyfully hearts and voices went up to God, in the beautiful Hindustani translation of the fine old hymn—

> O for a thousand tongues to sing
> My great Redeemer's praise,
> The glories of my God and King,
> The triumphs of His grace!

The experiences of these days at Lucknow were at once sweet and bitter. Sweet, because of loving welcomes from so many from whom she had been long severed, and because the greeting so often was, " How well you look." While these friends marvelled at the wonderful degree of health restored to Miss Reeed, they also rejoiced with her to recognise the hand of God in it, and to see how He was crowning His servant with loving kindness and tender mercies. Among the privileges most valued by her were interviews with the Rev. F. B. Meyer, to which reference is made in the introduction to this volume, and which were amongst the most inspiring of Mr. Meyer's experiences in India.

It is perhaps scarcely a matter for surprise that some showed a tendency to shrink from intimate association with one who had been for years " without the camp," owing to the taint of this most dreaded disease. Miss Reed frankly admitted the reasonableness of this attitude, and showed then, as always, the utmost solicitude for the safety of those with whom she was brought into close contact.

But the really "bitter" drop in her cup at this time was the pronouncement of a self-appointed body of four medical missionaries that the disease from which Miss Reed had so long suffered was not leprosy at all. While differing materially among themselves as to the real nature of the malady which for nine years or more had driven this brave soul into exile, they more than hinted their scepticism as to her ever having contracted this most dreaded of all diseases.

This opinion, however hastily arrived at, having been expressed by those possessing apparently some medical qualification, necessitates a re-statement of the evidence against which their hasty dictum was placed.

After many months of perplexity as to the nature of the complaint which first attacked the fore-finger, and subsequently further betrayed itself by a mark on the cheek, Miss Reed became at length convinced that leprosy had overtaken her. In this conviction she was confirmed by the decision of several eminent medical men, whose names will be recognized as those of leading authorities on this class of disease. Their opinions, it should be added, were arrived at in every instance after close personal examination. Miss Reed's case was diagnosed as one of undoubted leprosy by the following specialists, who examined her in the order named:—Dr. P. A. Morrow, of New York City, who is regarded by the profession in America as their highest authority; Sir Joseph Fayrer, K.C.S.I., M.D., and Mr. Jonathan Hutchinson, F.R.C.S., of London, both members of the Committee of the National Leprosy Fund; Dr. Chowsky, physician of the Bombay Leper Asylum;

and, lastly, Dr. Condon, a medical man of many years Indian experience. To this body of medical testimony may be added the decided opinion of Mr. Wellesley C. Bailey, the secretary and superintendent of the Mission to Lepers, who spent some days with Miss Reed in 1895, and felt no doubt whatever as to the nature of her disease. Mr. Bailey's opinion derives weight from his experience of work among lepers, and from many years special study of the subject.

To all this is to be added the fact that Miss Reed herself has never faltered in her conviction that she was "set apart" by personal experience of this most dreaded malady for work among its victims, and in that belief has submitted to eight years of almost entire isolation. When, moreover, some of her own descriptions of her symptons (already quoted) are borne in mind it will be obvious that but little importance can attach to an opinion formed upon a cursory and incomplete examination, and which was arrived at moreover, at a time when the distinctive symptoms were exceptionally abated and the general health remarkably good.

There is, however, another aspect, beside the medical one, to this question of the holding in check, or partial healing of the disease of leprosy in this remarkable case. When we remember that in the decided and unanimous opinion of the experts just named, Miss Reed has been for nine years suffering from a disease which in that period usually reduces its victims to a condition of hideous disfigurement, and when we also bear in mind that she has always declined the use of medical remedies, and that, nevertheless, she is now, and has been for many months past, in better general health than she frequently enjoyed in former years, we must admit that we have to do with a very unusual case indeed. And our wonder is enhanced by the fact that, at times, the outward symptoms so far subside as to be scarcely visible to an ordinary observer. But to the believer in the prayer of faith the explanation is not far to seek. There have been few missionaries for whom more constant prayer has been made than for Miss Reed. Since her story became more widely known, multitudes of Christian hearts, on both sides of the Atlantic, have offered up earnest petitions for strength, and, if it pleased God, even healing, to be granted to His servant. We cannot doubt, moreover, that Miss Reed's wonderful health is closely connected with the splendid spirit of consecration in which she accepted her cross of suffering and isolation. She has found an opiate for her own sorrow in devoted service among those whose sufferings far surpassed her own. The record of self-sacrificing labour contained in these pages, and the spirit of courage and consecration breathing through her letters, as well as the marked blessing vouchsafed to her efforts, are ample evidence that these many prayers have been graciously answered. But the wonderful health granted by the Divine Master to His faithful servant has brought with it some misunderstanding. Ardent and enthusiastic sympathizers have hastily jumped to the conclusion that their prayers have received the full answer for which they longed, and currency has been given to premature statements that Miss Reed has been healed. But the truth, as usual, lies between the two extremes. While the eager expectations of those who would fain see in Miss Reed an example of Divine cleansing from physical leprosy is not borne out by the facts, the scepticism of those who question that the disease has ever been present is still less justified.

THE PRAYER OF FAITH

But on this vital point it is as well that the subject of this biography should speak for herself, and my readers will be glad to peruse the following notes kindly contributed by Miss Reed, under date of June 9th, 1899. Referring to the doubts expressed by some who saw her when the outward marks of the disease were least evident, she writes :—

"It was a great grief to me, and to some of my nearest friends to realize that there are those even among our dear missionaries who prefer to doubt the existence of this most dreaded of all maladies rather than believe in what is by many called 'faith healing,' but what, in reality, this manifestation of God's keeping power is to *me*, viz., *Divine Health*.

"And so after that ordeal, which was followed by continuous trial for some months because of untrue and conflicting newspaper reports, I was enabled to make over to Him who cares and will not let me have too much to bear, this *new* phase of the trial of which we shall never know the full meaning here on earth. We *shall* know hereafter. Since my return home I have more than ever enjoyed singing with all my heart :—

> I leave it all with Jesus,
>   For He knows
> How to steal the bitter
>   From life's woes;
> How to gild the tear-drop
>   With His smile,
> Make the desert garden
>   Bloom awhile;
> When my weakness leaneth
>   On His might,
> All seems light.

"I found such a beautiful text only to-day. And because it has been, is being, and will continue to be verified to me I quote it: 'The heavens and the earth shall shake; but the Lord will be the hope (or the place of repair, or harbour) of His people and the strength of the Children of Israel (Joel iii. 16, with marginal reading). *That* is the secret! The Lord Himself our 'place of repair' and our harbour in times of storm. *His presence is Salvation.* Surely He hath borne our griefs, and carried our sorrows, and does not wish us to bear and carry them any more than the burden of sins.

"He gives me wondrous health and strength, far, far beyond what could be expected from a purely human standpoint. My general health has *never* been so good as it has been now for nearly a year past. Some of my friends have the impression from my appearance, and from the fact that Dr. Condon himself stated some months ago that he considered me 'practically' healed, that I have been 'made whole.' But *I know* that the 'seal' to the work of my Master's appointing here at Chandag Heights becomes *so* plainly *visible* at times that *no one* could doubt that disease still lingers in my system, though my finger does not now burst open as it did more than a score of times before 1898. (The italics are Miss Reed's).

"Who can fail to recognize the hand of God staying the malady in answer to the prayers of a multitude of Christian hearts bound by the blest tie of Christian love?

"Most humbly do I praise and thank God our Father and the Lord Jesus Christ our Saviour, the Fountain of life and health and peace, for marvellously improved health! 'He hath heard the voice of my (our) supplications .... my heart trusted in Him and *I am helped*; therefore my heart greatly rejoiceth, and with my song will I praise Him.'

"And now, in closing this very imperfect review of some experiences of these latter days, let me quote part of one of the chapters of the 'Book of Books,' which I committed to memory when a little girl. It made an indelible impression on my mind and heart, and—(dare I say it?)—upon my life also:—

"'NOT UNTO US, O LORD, NOT UNTO US, BUT UNTO THY NAME GIVE GLORY, FOR THY MERCY AND FOR THY TRUTH'S SAKE.'

"Wherefore should the heathen say, where is now their God?"

"BUT OUR GOD IS IN THE HEAVENS; HE HATH DONE WHATSOEVER HE HATH PLEASED.

"Their idols are silver and gold, the work of men's hands.

"'They have mouths, but they speak not; eyes have they, but they see not.' (Ps. cxv. 1-5.)

"Oh! how painfully true I have found it here, in this end of the earth, that 'they that make them are like unto them,' deaf to God's voice, and blind to His wondrous love until the entrance of His word, and the influence of His Holy Spirit enlighten and quicken those who are 'dead in trespasses and sins.'

"The dead praise not the Lord. . . . . .

"BUT WE WILL BLESS THE LORD FROM THIS TIME FORTH AND FOR EVERMORE. PRAISE THE LORD.

"Please pray for the salvation of the thousands of unsaved souls who have heard the call to come to Jesus and be saved. There are many all about us here who have *heard* the message of salvation, but are halting between two opinions. Please pray for them every time you think of us here in this out-post.

"As we pray and wait before the Lord, we come more and more to see with His eyes, and think His thoughts.

The flame of love burns more brightly, and we become missionary-hearted, with a heart somewhat akin to that of the first Great Missionary who came such a long, long journey to this lost and ruined world, 'that whosoever believeth on Him should not perish but have everlasting life.' May God help us all to assist in carrying the Gospel to perishing souls. May the Lord Himself teach us, and help us to be faithful in the 'ministry of intercession,' that His kingdom may come, and His will may be done on earth as it is in Heaven."

But few words remain to be added by the compiler of this volume, who would here gratefully acknowledge the spiritual stimulus he has often received from the life and the letters of Mary Reed, in the odd hours of a busy life, during which this labour of love has been fulfilled. At sundry times and in many places the work has been done, and to this the reader is asked in his charity to attribute the defects which a critical eye will readily discover.

Now the sum of what has been written is this:—A gentle and sensitive woman awakes suddenly to the appalling fact that she is a leper! Instantly her purpose is formed to devote herself to work among her fellow-sufferers. In unquestioning obedience to what she regards as the Divine voice, she journeys to the verge of the Himalayas. Near by is a small community of stricken people among whom Miss Reed is at once appointed to minister. Her labours have resulted in the admission, after careful testing, of 123 lepers into the Church of Christ. To this is to be added the provision of food, clothing, shelter, and relief for her large and growing flock, together with the comfort brought to their sad hearts by Christian sympathy and kindness. She has moreover acquired the extensive grounds, and supervised the erection, of what is now one of the finest leper asylums in the world. For nearly eight years she has laboured with unswerving purpose, in a degree of health that is amazing, and which all who believe in the power of prayer will gratefully recognize as Divinely bestowed.

This record of Mary Reed's life and work is issued in the hope that it may stimulate others to a consecration as complete as her own, and may, at the same time, call forth compassion and help for the many thousands of outcast lepers in our Indian Empire and other Eastern lands.

R. W. SIMPSON AND CO., LTD.,
THE RICHMOND PRESS, RICHMOND AND LONDON.

FOUNDED 1874.

THE MISSION TO LEPERS
IN INDIA AND THE EAST.

Objects of the Society.
To preach the Gospel of Jesus Christ to the Lepers.
To provide for their simple wants, and to relieve their dreadful sufferings.
To provide Homes for Lepers and for their untainted children.

Patroness:
THE MARCHIONESS OF DUFFERIN AND AVA.

President:
HIS GRACE THE LORD PRIMATE OF IRELAND.

Vice-Presidents:
VISCOUNT BANGOR.   SIR CHAS. ELLIOTT, K.C.S.I., LL.D.
REV. H. E. FOX, M.A., *Hon. Secretary, C.M.S.*
REV. W. PARK, M.A., *Convener of Foreign Missions, Irish Presbyterian Church.*
THE RIGHT HON. LORD POLWARTH.
REV. R. WARDLAW THOMPSON, *Foreign Secretary, L.M.S.*

What Money Will Do.
£4 supports a Child for 12 Months.
£5 supports a Leper for a Year.
£12 to £20 supports a Christian Teacher for a Year.
£150 to £300 will build an Asylum for Outcast Lepers.

Some of the Results.
Number of Stations of all kinds 53
Asylums entirely supported by the Society   20
Homes for Untainted Children 14

Total wholly or partially supported (about) 4,000
Christian Lepers in connection with the
    Society (about) 2,000

Hon. Secretary.—MISS C. E. PIM, Alma, Monkston, Co. Dublin.
Hon. Treasurer.—GRAVES S. EVES, ESQ., 18 Burlington Road, Dublin.
Secretary and Superintendent.—MR. WELLESLEY C. BAILEY, 17 Greenhill Place, Edinburgh.
Organizing and Deputation Secretary.—MR. JOHN JACKSON, Exeter Hall, Strand, London, W.C.

The Mission to Lepers.

WHILE the unsectarian character of the Society will will be inferred from the names of its office-bearers, it may be stated that the work is done in co-operation with the agents of twenty other Societies, including THE CHURCH MISSIONARY, THE BAPTIST, THE LONDON, THE WESLEYAN, AND SEVERAL PRESBYTERIAN MISSIONARY SOCIETIES. The work being carried on, or supervised, by Missionaries already on the spot, assisted in many instances by native helpers, the Committee are enabled to devote THE LARGEST POSSIBLE AMOUNT OF THE FUNDS TO THE DIRECT BENEFIT OF THE LEPERS.

Official Testimony.

His Honour the Lieutenant-Governor of Bengal, on a recent visit to the Asylum at Purulia, wrote in the Visitors' Book:— "I have been greatly impressed by my visit to this Asylum. It has now upwards of 500 inmates, and the sight of so great a company of stricken people would have been most distressing had it not been for the surprising contentment of their bearing. No leper is sent by the authorities, and no wall prevents an inmate from leaving, and yet the numbers rapidly grow! Evidence of the constant kindness and sympathy with which the poor creatures are treated! I have seen no more truly benevolent work in India than this."

The Society's Publications.

The Lepers of our Indian Empire. By WELLESLEY C. BAILEY. Bound in cloth, illustrated. Nett price, 2s.

A Visit to Leper Asylums in India and Burma. By WELLESLEY C. BAILEY. Paper covers, illustrated. Price 6d.

The Story of the Mission to Lepers. By H. S. CARSON, author of "From Loom to Lawyer's Gown." Illustrated. Price 3d.

Sons of Affliction. By JOHN JACKSON. Just published. Illustrated. Price 1d.

Mandalay Asylum. By ERIC DANKS, Esq., B.A., I.C.S. Just published, illustrated. Price 1d.

THE QUARTERLY MAGAZINE:
"WITHOUT THE CAMP."
Illustrated and containing letters from Missionaries and accounts of their work. To any address, post free, 6d. per annum.
To be obtained from any of the Secretaries.

www.ingramcontent.com/pod-product-compliance
Lightning Source LLC
Chambersburg PA
CBHW031334160426
43196CB00007B/685